SEVEN
Secrets
TO UNFOLDING
Destiny

MARK CHIRONNA

DESTINY IMAGE® PUBLISHERS, INC.

P.O. Box 310, Shippensburg, PA 17257-0310

"Speaking to the Purposes of God for This Generation and for the Generations to Come."

This book and all other Destiny Image, Revival Press, MercyPlace, Fresh Bread, Destiny Image Fiction, and Treasure House books are available at Christian bookstores and distributors worldwide.

For a U.S. bookstore nearest you, call 1-800-722-6774.

For more information on foreign distributors, call 717-532-3040.

Reach us on the Internet: www.destinyimage.com.

ISBN 13 Trade Paper: 978-0-7684-3206-0
ISBN 13 Hardcover: 978-0-7684-3369-2
ISBN 13 Large Print: 978-0-7684-3370-8
ISBN 13 E-book: 978-0-7684-9134-0

For Worldwide Distribution, Printed in the U.S.A.

2 3 4 5 6 7 8 9 10 11 / 13 12 11 10

Endorsements

Thousands of years ago, Yahweh declared to a fledgling young preacher three incredible truths about his life *before* he was even born: "I knew you." "I consecrated you." "I appointed you." Dr. Chironna masterfully guides his readers on the journey to discover their destination and how to cooperate with their *internal* destiny that will unfold their *eternal* destiny.

Bishop Joseph L. Garlington Sr.

In my opinion, Dr. Mark Chironna is the leading author on the subject of the prophetic and specifically on destiny. I have personally learned much from his many insights, and Mark has assisted me in avoiding the pitfalls that I would've encountered on my journey to my destiny. Your destiny is not lost, it's waiting for you, and Dr. Chironna's skill in explaining the process in relevant language makes the journey on earth so much more interesting. Thank you, Mark, for taking the time to pen your brilliance to paper. If you are serious about receiving and possessing your allotted portion in the Kingdom with the least hindrance, then *Seven Secrets to Unfolding Destiny* is a must!

Kim Clement

My friend Mark Chironna has the unique ability to take a difficult subject and make it easy to understand. Destiny is one of those concepts that we try to grasp but always seems just out of reach. As I read this latest book from Mark, I realized that it was not only well-written, but that I couldn't put it down. I was learning something powerful about understanding my own destiny. That's awesome! As you read this book, prepare for an exciting acceleration in the race toward your future.

Pastor Mike Hayes

There are a few select individuals uniquely gifted to articulate the necessary tools for access to that elusive dimension called destiny. Mark Chironna has once again focused our attention on the abilities all of us possess. *Seven Secrets to Unfolding Destiny* takes you by the hand and directs you toward attaining your dreams, aspirations, and goals. Inspiring, informative, and entertaining, it is a must-read.

David G. Evans, Pastor, Advisor, Entrepreneur, and
Author of *Healed Without Scars* and *Dare to Be a Man*

Dr. Mark Chironna is one of the foremost instructors in helping people reach their God-given destiny. This newest book is a road map to living a life of abundance and blessing.

I highly recommend it to everyone who wants to achieve all that God has for them.

Benny Perez, Lead Pastor
www.thechurchlv.com

To call Dr. Mark Chironna's book, *Seven Secrets to Unfolding Destiny*, a self-help guide would be insulting. The truth is it's so much more. This is the most insightful, intelligent, on-target, and well-written book I have ever read about how to discover and follow your destiny—and how to live an authentic life. I love that it also reveals, so simply and so lyrically, how to become a whole person who vibrates with purpose and passion, connects easily with other people, and is in tune with life's pauses, rhythms, and discords. It goes to deep places and will take you there, too. Please, please read it. But I must caution you: If you do, you will never be the same—you'll know all the secrets to an abundant life. And believe me, you won't want to live without them.

Simon T. Bailey
Author of Release Your Brilliance

In *Seven Secrets to Unfolding Destiny*, Dr. Chironna exposes limiting belief systems while extinguishing excuses that reside in so many hearts. You will finish this book inspired, impacted, and thirsty to explore your potential and accomplish the impossible in any environment.

Dominic Russo
Dominic Russo Ministries

Dr. Chironna is one of the premiere leaders in the country who is helping people walk the path of purpose and ultimately fulfill their destiny. This book is a great resource.

Dr. Teresa Hairston
Gospel Today Magazine

It is always a privilege and an honor to comment on my dear friend, Mark Chironna—a man who is on the cutting edge of what the Lord is doing and saying to the Body of Christ and who has the character and experience to help many people reach their purpose and destiny. Many have no idea where they came from or where they are going—their destiny—but in this book, Dr. Chironna provides the revelation to understand why we are here and the secrets of how to unfold our God-given destiny. I highly recommend this book. It will certainly touch you and change your life. I admire and respect Dr. Chironna and his ministry—for his integrity and expertise in showing us how to experience and discover our destiny in Jesus Christ.

Apostle Guillermo Maldonado

Table of Contents

PART III
Unpack the Secrets
(How to Unfold Destiny Daily)

Preface

THE DESTINY-FULFILLED LIFE. Most dream of it. Some live in inspired pursuit of it. Relatively few experience it fully. In fact, vast numbers have surrendered in seeming defeat so long ago that they no longer believe it is even possible.

Yet, no matter how dormant that thoughts of unfolding destiny become, destiny awaits!

Meanwhile, the world keeps turning. In the budding twenty-first century, events have altered our sense of how things work, who is safe, and what we can expect in the future. Financial rumblings produce widespread uncertainty. Economic fallout has altered once-clear perceptions of who's who. Powerful executives have had their sails trimmed; famously affluent people have seen their fortunes evaporate; some of the world's largest companies have disappeared or have downsized to a degree unimaginable until now.

The rejiggering of paradigms and power structures tempts many of us to assume that, even if destiny awaits us, the timing is all wrong. For large numbers of people, caution and retreat are the order of the day. Forward pursuits are shelved in resignation until the dust settles. Dreams are postponed—indefinitely.

Well, not for everybody. Historically, uncertain times present uncommon opportunities to shoot hoops with the world's players and put some points on the scoreboard. Shifting sands can level the playing field just enough to give outsiders new chances to compete.

What of that? Are previously nonexistent destiny opportunities available to the "unlikely" among us? Are we living in a time in which every good idea can launch a dream come true? Do those who believe themselves to be excluded from the ranks of the destiny-fulfilled suddenly have a shot at greatness?

My response is, "Yes and no."

"That's no response at all!" you cry. "How does someone so indecisive manage to write books?"

My answer sounds indecisive; but it's not. Will new opportunities arise? Sure. Every transition uncovers new prospects for those who are alert to them. But it's equally true that some traditional opportunities will disappear. Just ask the United States Postal Service how that equation works. As technological advancements create new methods and opportunities in cyberspace, "snail mail" appears headed for obsolescence, and letter carriers are in less demand.

As for the potential of good ideas to produce phenomenal outcomes—yes!—that potential is as strong as ever. Some are convinced that the potential is *greater* than ever. But that's not really news; the potential has *always* been there. For those determined to turn lemons into lemonade, opportunity is found in unlikely places. Entrepreneurs often run their ideas up flimsy flagpoles, and many watch their dreams come true.

Meanwhile, the reticent among us adopt a "someday" mentality; they keep great ideas tucked safely under the mattress waiting for the day when circumstances are perfectly ripe. Some cautious folks will find a later wave to ride to success. Many others will discover that the shelf life of their big idea has expired and someone else has taken their money to the bank.

And what about those who see themselves as being stuck on the outside looking in? They generally fall into two camps. In one camp are those who learn a powerful truth: Greatness doesn't come from *out there*; greatness is already *within* us. At some point they discover that a life of fulfilled destiny is the outcome for which they were designed. They recognize, whether by revelation or experience, that financial tremors and changing geo-political climates cannot thwart the fulfillment of individual destinies…unless the destined surrender.

In the opposite camp, life is on hold. These wait-and-see campers are convinced that the wrong climate has shoved them farther outside the fence than they were before. Intimidated by the "what ifs" of life, their dreams gradually slip out of reach. Goals are pushed back. One day blends into the next, and hope fades with every sunset.

So, while my answer may have seemed flippant, the premise of the questions was faulty; it assumed that destiny is something for which you wait with one finger raised to detect the direction of the wind and one hand digging like crazy for just enough to keep you going until the current wind blows over.

The future, however, isn't something you wait for; it's something you help create. It is a function, in part, of your imagination and your willingness to allow your imagination to accomplish its purpose.

Your dreams, thoughts, wishes, and ideas are more powerful than you might believe. The world has always been an equal-opportunity environment—not necessarily a place of equal ease or equal results, but a massive field of destiny treasures waiting to be unearthed by people of every ilk. Regardless of where you began, where you have been, or whom your parents are—regardless of how high you have soared in the past or how far you have fallen, a life of destiny fulfillment is your birthright; it is a state of being that is available to everyone.

Yes—everyone.

While it is true that multitudes never attain their dreams, it is also true that everyone aspires to do so. This hope is written in our DNA and, when it is given place, greatness results. History proves it. Rags-to-riches stories and accounts of profound accomplishment—cures for plagues, the preservation of imperiled nations, the overcoming of disability—abound even among those whose upward trajectory seemed unlikely:

Jonas Salk, a medical researcher who developed the first effective polio vaccine, was the child of immigrants who had no formal education.[1]

Abraham Lincoln's parents were born of "undistinguished" families.[2]

At the age of six, Helen Keller was "a half-wild, deaf and blind girl."[3]

Why were these lives so rich, both in the accomplishment of destiny and in their impact upon the rest of us? It is because every human being is endued with immeasurable potential and value. This truth compelled me to write this book. Observations, revelations, and experiences gathered over a lifetime of study have convinced me that every one of us is eligible for success in the largest sense of the word.

"So," you ask, "if *everyone* is eligible for unfolding destiny, why is this book about *secrets?*"

The answer begins with part of my working definition of the word *secret*: A secret is something that is set apart, withdrawn, and hidden. (I will talk more about this definition later.)

Secrets are hidden, yet not out of reach. Often, the most powerful secrets are hidden from us by nothing more than the lack of awareness that they exist or apply to our lives. Sometimes, the information we need is obscured from view by what we think we know or by what we believe to be true—about ourselves, about others, about where we fit in this world.

The goal of this book is to pierce the veil, reveal the secrets, and unfold the future each of us was created to live. The secrets of unfolding destiny—and destiny itself—are not just for a select few.

They are for you!

ENDNOTES

1. The Academy of Achievement, "Jonas Salk Biography," http://www.achievement.org/autodoc/page/sal0bio-1 (accessed June 24, 2009).

2. The White House, "Abraham Lincoln," http://www. whitehouse.gov/about/presidents/AbrahamLincoln/ (accessed June 24, 2009).

3. Helen Keller's Birthplace, "Helen Keller Biography," http://www.helenkellerbirthplace.org/helenkellerbio /helen_keller_birthplace2_bio.htm (accessed June 24, 2009).

PART

I

Suit Up to Move Forward

(How to "Dress" for Conscious Living)

CHAPTER ONE

Saddle Up and Ride

TO GET WHERE YOU want to go, you have to do something you've never done. Your future isn't something you wait for. It is something you help create with your imagination. You are equipped to bring into existence what has never existed before. You are a unique creative being; therefore your desires and their expression are more powerful than you think possible. Don't wait for your future to show up. Go out and meet it. Determine to create a world and make a world of difference.[1]

Whether your past was wonderful or has left you wanting, your future is yours, and it is straight ahead. No, you needn't wonder and wait for it. Yes, you *can* go out and meet it—head-on, large, and in charge!

You are reading this page. That says two things about you: First, you have a sense of destiny. Second, it is important to you. Yet, it says more; it tells me that you are finished with a wait-and-see lifestyle. You want to live in The Zone—the tangible but not necessarily physical place where the destiny engine fires on all cylinders and thrusts you forward—not just anywhere, but to a place with your name on it.

Because you are no longer content to coast into the future, you find yourself asking the same big-picture questions people have asked throughout the eons:

"Who am I, really?"

"Where am I headed, and why?"

"What is the essential meaning of my life and how can I live my purpose—fully, joyfully, and without compromise?"

Everyone asks these questions at one time or another. Asking them is good; but asking is not enough. To find the kind of life you know in your gut you were born to live, you must be willing to dig for the answers, even when the mining gets messy, which it will. Before you reach for the white gloves, let me assure you of this: any mess you make will be worth it. Well worth it.

So, you are here. Whatever "here" looks like, it is your Point A. You know you are headed someplace out "there." We'll call it Point B. It's a better place (no one hopes for things to get worse, right?), but some of the blanks are yet to be filled in. That's exactly as it should be; this process starts with questions, not answers. The road between Points A and B isn't 100 percent clear. All you need to know right now is that there *is* a road.

Most of what you know is already behind you. If your experience is anything like mine, it has probably shown you that getting from

Point A to Point B is not merely a matter of straight lines, time, and distance. Formulas are for mathematics; they serve their purpose, but this isn't one of them.

No, your quest is more consequential than that. That's obvious from the emotions it engenders. We are preparing to explore something deep and deeply meaningful. Once you dig your way to the core and hold up to the light the treasures you unearth, your life will be in a place of empowerment it has never been before. It will be a place where truth-based thoughts and realities are so clearly linked as to be nearly inseparable and virtually unstoppable.

The real distance between where you are now and the place of unfolded destiny is not calculated in feet or days or decades; it is measured in the arrangement of your thoughts and the extent to which they serve to integrate the various parts of your life in harmony with your destiny.

Regardless of the circumstances of your life at this moment—yes, even if all hell has broken loose in your world—your destiny remains within eyeshot and earshot of Point A. In fact, it is no farther from your reach than your imagination can take you.

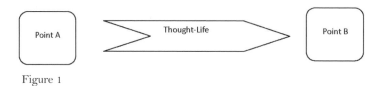

Figure 1

YOU ARE A CREATIVE BEING

When I talk about imagination, I'm not talking about pipe dreams or conjuring; I'm referring to authentic creativity, the kind of out-of-the-box living that makes most people uncomfortable, not only with creative thinkers, but mostly with themselves.

Comfort zones are just that: comfortable. They are environments we erect to cushion us from the blunt force of change. Comfort zones justify our aversion to risk and compel us to shrink back from greatness. From within these airtight bubbles, we tend to discredit other's dreams and even our own; we respond with sweeping judgments saying, "It's just your imagination." Instead of being supportive of creative endeavors, we trample the first green shoots of future triumphs.

Your creative bent as a human being is your most valuable feature. It is designed to produce unfathomable results. Your imagination is a faculty that enables you to envision—and *create*—something other than what already exists. Without it, you would be doomed to stagnation and at the mercy of every circumstance in your sphere. Absent the power of imagination, you would be as limited as a caged canary, ever waiting for someone to fill your seed cup and always subject to the outside forces controlling your world.

Human beings were not designed for such limitations. We are created beings who possess an unlimited capacity to create. For biological parents, the idea of creating often sparks memories of the conception and birth of a child. *Procreation* is perhaps the most awe-inspiring generative capacity we possess. Yet, in the end, it is not *our* creativity that determines the conception or birth characteristics of our children.

The creativity I'm talking about is unique to each individual. It is expressed through ideas. It is manifested when ideas become reality. The process of creation begins in the thought realm. In fact, everything we do in life begins with a conscious or unconscious thought. These thoughts inspire choices; we call these choices *actions*. Actions then lead to outcomes. The outcomes we experience are the result of the actions we take or fail to take.

We'll talk about this more in a later chapter; the important point now is that our actions and outcomes begin in our thinking.

Thinking and creativity are highly individual activities. A simple imaginary experiment demonstrates this idea. Imagine that you have gathered 50 artists in a room with 50 easels. Now imagine that each artist has been supplied with an identical palette and brushes of identical width and texture. Projected on a large screen is a photograph of a landscape. The artists are asked to recreate the landscape on canvas in a set period of time, using all of the colors and brushes provided.

When time is up, the artists drop their brushes. You quickly discover that 50 painters have created 50 unique interpretations of a single scene. Each has approached the various elements of the landscape differently: their color choices vary; their emphases on literal and abstract representation differ; focal points are treated uniquely.

Each painter has told the visual story in a distinctive way. This is partly due to the fact that training, techniques, and levels of talent are not uniform. But the differences in outcome also have to do with the intrinsic individuality of each artist. The painters have brought to the assignment their own creative tendencies and their unreplicated perspectives. Although they all worked from the same image, each saw it from a different emotional and aesthetic point of view. Therefore each artist ascribed to the scene a meaning of his or her own.

POINT A AND PERCEPTION

Artists are creative and unique, but so are those who view art. Ask ten people who have seen the *Mona Lisa* to describe the painting and its emotional, intellectual, and spiritual impact. You guessed it: you will get ten different answers.

No two people view the world through the same lens. Part of the reason we find art so compelling is because it invites us to bring our individuality to the interpretation. We are able to find something in the art that connects with our own lives. We see what the artist put into the work, but what we take from it—our perception of it—is completely individual.

Perceptions about *self* and others play an enormous role in the unfolding of destiny. Whether we do so consciously or not, we see the world through the prism of life learning and experiences. We form in advance nearly ironclad opinions of how things will or should turn out. Inwardly, we believe in a particular destiny outcome; whether consciously or not, we already believe that we can or cannot achieve destiny fulfillment.

Others form similarly ironclad opinions about us. For better or worse, we often accept these viewpoints as truth. A well-known biblical account illustrates my point. Jesus and His disciples came upon a man who was blind from birth. Immediately, Jesus' disciples asked, *"Who sinned, this man or his parents, that he would be born blind?"*[2]

These men were intent on finding meaning in the man's disability. Instead of feeling compassion for him, they began to categorize him as someone who deserved to be blind for one reason or another. Rather than feel his pain, they elevated themselves above him in their own thinking and tried to frame his misfortune as something that could not have happened to them.

How many times had the blind man heard such words, and how might those words have affected his opinions of himself as a human being? His story was not private; his condition was well known, and his begging was part of the daily public scene. The disciples' unkindness wasn't the first he'd heard. In our modern lingo, we wonder whether his self-esteem was damaged by the remarks of passersby. Did he internalize the idea of blindness as a personal failure? Or did he manage to separate the fact that he was a man—a valuable human being by dint of having been born—from the fact that he happened to be a *blind* man?

Your sense of who you are is framed in your thinking and affected by many internal and external factors. In every endeavor, moment by moment, whether on the job, in your relationships, or in the general conduct of your life, you see yourself as being a certain way and you use language to describe the person you perceive yourself to be. Whether consciously or unconsciously, you describe yourself as being:

- Able or unable
- Likely or unlikely
- Wanted or unwanted
- Blessed or cursed
- Worthy or unworthy

Regardless of how your perceptions of self were formed, they serve to define you. They also contribute to the perceptions of others and influence their behavior toward you. If you are not clear as to your authentic identity, your internal language and their audible words will confine you to perceptions that essentially represent the past. Uncontested thoughts and words will restrict you from moving forward.

We will examine the role of perceptions in the unfolding of destiny. For now, we can agree that our perceptions (and misconceptions) about self-concept, self-worth, and self-esteem are not only key to our childhood development, but also to the quality of our adult lives. Perceptions can give free rein to a healthy sense of imagination or build strongholds to encase us in what is essentially misinformation.

Misinformation about identity can inadvertently become the recurring headline of our lives and hinder our creativity in unfolding destiny. There is good news, however: we can learn to take accurate stock of our perceptions and adjust our thought patterns accordingly. When we do so, we change the internal playing field of life. This in turn recalibrates our outcomes. Even subtle shifts in our perceptions can transform the world around us.

Snapshots of *Self*

Until we develop the discipline to question our perceptions and base them on truth, we will continue to develop confused pictures of self. Let's lay the groundwork for future discussions of three of these snapshots by establishing working definitions for them. They are *self-concept, self-esteem,* and *self-worth.*

Your self-concept is your global evaluation of who you perceive yourself to be. Self-concept is a kind of big-picture checklist that covers such details as your role in society, your status, and other overarching characteristics of your person. Some of these features are measured against so-called *norms.* Your self-concept might be stated this way: *I am a married Hispanic woman, the mother of three, and a schoolteacher. I am an athletic person who runs the marathon each year. I am successful in my profession and expect career advancement in coming years.*

> ### self-concept *noun:*
> An individual's assessment of his or her status on a single trait or on many human dimensions using societal or personal norms as criteria.[3]

26

The term *low self-esteem* is widely used in our culture, especially when discussing emotional development, the breakdown of the family, and other types of dysfunction springing from abuse, the worship of celebrity, and other societal issues. *Self-esteem* as a snapshot of self is evaluated and experienced at an affective level. In other words, it involves feelings. Your self-esteem is both an inherent trait and a skill that can be learned. It can be described as the degree to which your view of self is favorable. Aspects of self-esteem can be reflected in characteristics such as self-confidence and the sense of security.

> ### self-esteem *noun*:
>
> A realistic respect for or favorable impression of oneself; self-respect.[4]

Self-worth is a value statement. It is formulated through the use of your cognitive skills. The sense of self-worth expresses the extent to which you believe you are deserving of being respected by others and by yourself. Your self-worth is your perceived value as a person based on what you believe or believe you know about yourself. This perception is very closely linked to your self-esteem.

> ### self-worth *noun*:
>
> The sense of one's own value or worth as a person...[5]

Do you remember the disciples' assumptions about the blind man? Their need to categorize him and ascribe blame for his condition was rooted in their own confusion about self-concept, self-esteem, and self-worth. They assumed the concept of his blindness was linked to his esteem as an individual. Instead of esteeming him as a human being apart from anyone else, they tried to evaluate him using their own snapshots of self as their standards of measurement. They assumed he was different from them (blind when they were not) because of something untoward he had done. They therefore assumed that his worth was compromised when, in fact, his worth was not dependent on his performance or on his physical attributes. His worth was inherent in his humanness.

Others often fail to recognize our inherent worth. Yet, we are the ones who most often devalue ourselves. We develop self-concepts that fall far short of who we really are. Our self-esteem may have been damaged by others, but we compound our emotional injuries by accepting and institutionalizing other people's assessments of us. Too often, we fail to remember that, if we were born into this world (*whatever* the circumstances of our birth), we have immeasurable, indelible worth. We are the most valuable of all created beings.

Why are our views of self so important, and why is it necessary to test their validity? Simply stated, we will never see life's bigger picture until we see ourselves accurately. Only then can we see where we belong and what we were created to do. Only with a truth-based picture of ourselves can we flourish to our fullest potential.

The significance goes beyond our lives: the fulfillment of our potential finds its fullest expression in the benefit we bring to others. We are here to create solutions to problems great and small; we are prospective benefactors to individuals, societies, and noble causes.

WHAT DOES IT ALL MEAN?

At the heart of our questions is the search that drives us: it is the quest for meaning. It is a fundamental human need at the root of our highest pursuits. It is also the reason for baser behaviors such as rubbernecking at a highway crash site. We stare aghast at these awful scenes trying to understand why we are driving by unscathed while the lives of others are interrupted or abruptly ended.

Neurologist, psychiatrist, and Holocaust survivor Viktor Frankl explains our search for meaning this way:

> Man's search for meaning is the primary motivation in his life and not a "secondary rationalization" of instinctual drives. This meaning is unique and specific in that it must and can be fulfilled by him alone; only then does it achieve a significance, which will satisfy his own *will* to meaning.[6]

We are natural born meaning-makers. Have you ever noticed your irritation when someone says or does something that, in your mind, makes no sense? How do you respond? Do you force the issue by demanding an explanation, or do you mull over it again and again searching for a window into the offender's train of thought?

We are critical thinkers, and meaning is crucial to our thought processes. Typically, when something fails to make obvious sense, we examine it more closely until it does or until we move on. This search for meaning is connected to our identity as spiritual beings. Regardless of the position you take on faith, religion, and deity, you naturally seek for meaning that extends beyond yourself. We all desire to understand our connection to something bigger and less fleeting than our brief lives and physical limitations.

When this deep, essential need for meaning goes unmet, we begin to feel shallow, empty, useless, powerless, and inadequate. Moods swing toward the negative, not briefly, but for long periods of time. Feelings of boredom, frustration, and depression replace the sense of adventure, accomplishment, and joy that connectedness to meaning generates.

Meaning is an essential ingredient for unfolding destiny.

LANGUAGE AND MEANING

Language gives form to our thoughts. We use language to convey ideas and meaning to others. Language is one of the vehicles by which we express our inherent creativity. Therefore, our words are far more than combinations of letters and sounds or disposable expressions of thought.

The animal kingdom communicates with sound. Dolphins convey information through a system of sounds understood by other dolphins and studied by the scientific community. If you own a dog, you know that you can teach him to respond to specific commands. He is also capable of connecting a limited number of words to certain objects.

Although your dog fetches your slippers and dolphins convey warnings of danger and other types of information, they cannot accomplish what you can: they cannot create or control reality with language. They can express themselves to a degree, but they cannot effect transformation in the world around them.

Human language is generative. In other words, it is "capable of producing or creating."[7] Language affects outcomes in your life. The story of the blind man goes on to explain that his neighbors had a particular concept of him: they *previously saw him as a beggar.*[8]

When the man's sight was restored,[9] the townspeople had to adjust their thinking in response to his newfound abilities.

Blindness was only part of the challenge faced by this man over his lifetime. Equally formidable was the deck of words stacked against him. The neighbors saw him as a beggar, and the disciples saw him as a sinner to blame for his own blindness. We don't know much else about this man's life story, but we can say that, unless he was equipped with a healthy self-concept, self-esteem, and self-worth, the blistering words of others could easily have suppressed his potential and steered him away from his unfolding destiny.

Language is powerful; it is designed to be used by us to create reality. The power of language cuts both ways: it can enforce the presence of strongholds (the invisible, self-limiting borders we accept or enforce around our lives); or it can release the untapped potential that is ready to surge from within.

MEANING DETERMINES PURPOSE

The search for meaning activates the opening of new doors of understanding and effectiveness. When you discover the meaning of something, you can correctly evaluate its importance and potential applications. Because you see it in context, you can identify its *purpose*.

Meaning determines purpose. Consider the life of Florence Nightingale. Born into a wealthy family in 1820, Florence was expected to cultivate a strong social and domestic life. Instead, she sought an unacceptable path for women of her social status: she desired to become a nurse. Mid-nineteenth-century nursing was a far different profession than it is today. When Nightingale began her career, hospitals were substandard, bacteria-infested places where people were too often sent to die without real care.

Florence's family opposed her plan. She persevered in her purpose and is credited with organizing a team of nurses to serve in the Crimean War. She is also well-known for bringing systemic reform to nursing practices and hospital administration, laying the groundwork for modern hospital care.

Florence Nightingale's resistance of societal norms was meaningful. Her insistence on a particular path was inspired. It was an expression of the purpose for which she was created. It led to the fulfillment of her destiny and it redounded to the betterment of humankind.

Florence Nightingale discovered meaning in her life and allowed it to determine her purpose. Her sense of purpose then yielded the courage she would need to challenge paradigms, withstand opposition, and endure hardship. At some point, Nightingale realized that she was not a freak of nature or an accidental rebel. She was a magnificent creation, skillfully crafted by her Maker. She did not allow herself to be defined by circumstances, perceived limitations, or other people's expectations. Instead she saw herself as part of something bigger than she.

Nothing about you is an accident, either. Whether or not you believe it at this moment, you are one of a kind, a grand design with all the human potential of Florence Nightingale, Bill Gates, or Thomas Edison. Wherever you are, Point B is within reach. Your imagination is ready to take you there. Take a deep breath and relax. Drop your guard enough to challenge old thoughts and entertain new ones. Allow this to be a season of freedom to discover new things.

Realize that you already believe some things about yourself, your purpose, your potential. Ask yourself what they are and put them to the truth test. Be willing to step outside the boundaries of your established thinking. Prepare to uncover and then discard self-limiting thoughts so that you can step into a place of reward and fulfillment you've never experienced before.

Saddle up; we're leaving Point A.

ENDNOTES

1. Mark J. Chironna, Ph.D., *The Seven Secrets of Unfolding Destiny* (lecture paraphrase, The Master's Touch International Church, Longwood, FL, January 26, 2007).

2. John 9:2.

3. "Self-concept," Dictionary.com. *The American Heritage® Stedman's Medical Dictionary* (Houghton Mifflin Company), http://dictionary.reference.com/browse/self-concept (accessed June 29, 2009).

4. "Self-esteem," Dictionary.com, Dictionary.com Unabridged, v. 1.1 (Random House, Inc.), http://dictionary.reference.com/browse/self-esteem (accessed June 30, 2009).

5. "Self-worth," Dictionary.com, Dictionary.com Unabridged, v. 1.1 (Random House, Inc.), http://dictionary.reference.com/browse/self-worth (accessed June 30, 2009).

6. Viktor Frankl, *Man's Search for Meaning* (Boston: Beacon Press, 1992), 105, http://books.google.com/books?id=K2AvZmco3E0C&dq=man's+search+for+meaning+victor+frankl&printsec=frontcover&source=bl&ots=cKnkG1CAgh&sig=EWojeCGMMlXdMUeOoppa8ajTUfY&hl=en&ei=uEFBSrOoH4j2sQPW8tDxCA&sa=X&oi=book_result&ct=result&resnum=5 (accessed June 30, 2009).

7. "Generative," Dictionary.com, Dictionary.com Unabridged, v. 1.1 (Random House, Inc.), http://dictionary.reference.com/browse/generative (accessed June 30, 2009).

8. John 9:8.

9. John 9:7.

UNFOLD YOUR DESTINY

1. Take a few moments to consider three personal goals you wish to accomplish as you read this book.

2. Write down your goals in the space provided.

CHAPTER TWO

Destiny Certain

"The best way to predict the future is to invent it."
—Alan Kay

COMPUTER SCIENTIST ALAN KAY has done more than talk about inventing the future; he has done it. Every time you boot up your desktop or laptop computer and double-click an icon, you inhabit the future that Alan Kay helped to create. Just a few sentences about Kay's life serve up a heaping portion of his global impact:

> Alan Kay has been called the father of the personal computer in acknowledgment of his many contributions to the field of personal computing. His concept of the Dynabook lap-top computer was the inspiration of Alto,

a forerunner of the Apple and Macintosh computers. Kay
also pioneered the use of icons and windows....[1]

We know that computers have transformed communications;
industrial methods; scientific research; the handling of money; the
operation of world markets; the prosecution of wars; the running of
political campaigns; the management of local, national, and international security; transportation; and more.

Alan Kay was in the minority of early computer scientists who
believed that computers would be widely used. His belief drove
him to explore practical ways to put the power of computing in
the hands of everyday people. The implications were, and continue to be, monumental.

How many areas of *your* personal life are affected by computers?
Did you use a computer at work today? Send an electronic message
to your senator? Pay your mortgage online? Write a few pages of
your thesis? Research a medical condition affecting your family? Find
your dream home? Book travel plans? Send a digital photo album to
loved ones?

Kay's innovations, like all innovations, were processed in the
human imagination, not by accident, but by providential design. The
contributions he has made to society are part of the unfolding of his
destiny. His unique giftings, including strengths in science and
mathematics, enabled him to advance the world's digital revolution.
His ways of thinking empowered him to synthesize knowledge and
imagination to create technological realities.

Alan Kay pursued his beliefs, despite the naysayers. He didn't
wait for the future; he created it.

THE NUTS AND BOLTS OF DESTINY

The word *destiny* is bantered around a lot. Too often, destiny is viewed as a topic too ethereal to be approachable. We can demystify the topic with clear language. Let's start with a working definition of the word so central to our discussion:

Destiny is the powerful and irresistible force of something foreordained.[2] Destiny evokes your greatness and your noble course in life and manifests your God-given grand design. Your destiny encompasses every area of your life from the inside out. It includes your spiritual, vocational, psychological, social, physical, financial, and family life.

---

destiny *noun*:

1. something to which a person or thing is destined.

2. a predetermined course of events often held to be an irresistible power or agency.

For Alan Kay, destiny was powerful and irresistible. He had been traveling another path altogether when he was drawn into his unfolding destiny through a series of circumstances:

> …[Kay] relied on his musical talents to make a living in Denver playing jazz clubs and giving guitar lessons. But he found another **latent talent** when he joined the Air Force and performed well on a computer programming aptitude test. He was sent to work on an IBM 1401 by the U.S. Air Force[3] (emphasis added).

Kay's latent talent had been there all along; the Air Force simply uncovered it. In doing so, they unleashed the dynamics of destiny and launched Kay into his element, an environment in which his destiny would gradually unfold. His purpose would be revealed, opened to view, and spread out for all to see.

---

unfold *verb*:

1. to bring out of a folded state; spread or open out: *Unfold your arms.*
2. to spread out or lay open to view.
3. to reveal or display.
4. to reveal or disclose in words, esp. by careful or systematic exposition; set forth; explain.[4]

This unfolding of destiny was foreordained; it is the reason Kay's talent existed in the first place. When something is foreordained, it is appointed, determined, decreed, or settled beforehand; it is predetermined—designated, assigned, and dedicated in advance.

---

foreordain *verb*:

1. to ordain or appoint beforehand
2. to predestine; predetermine[5]

Consider the words of Joseph Campbell, an academic known for his studies of comparative religion and mythology:

If you follow your bliss, you put yourself on a kind of track that has been there all the while, waiting for you, and the life that you ought to be living is the one you are living. Wherever you are—if you are following your bliss, you are enjoying that refreshment, that life within you, all the time.[6]

Alan Kay found himself on the track that had been there all along. His work not only contributed to societal transformation; it also enriched his own life through meaningful scientific pursuit, achievement, and reward. The unfolding of destiny evoked Kay's greatness and his noble course in life and manifested his God-given grand design.

Kay's unfolding destiny impacted other areas of his life. But this is not a book about Alan Kay. It's a book about you. Imagine yourself in the full-blown pursuit of your dream. To borrow Campbell's language, how would your spiritual, vocational, psychological, social, physical, financial, and family life be refreshed by following your bliss?

YOUR DESTINY ENCODED

You have a destiny path that already exists. It can be compared to the Israelites' path through the Red Sea: nobody knew it was there until the sea parted and the path was revealed. With the Egyptian army at their backs and the Red Sea ahead, there seemed no way out for the Israelites (see Ps. 77:19-20). Once the exit was exposed, however, the meaning of the path across the Red Sea became clear. For the hunted, the meaning was freedom.

Similarly, the path of your unfolded destiny is already in place, waiting to be discovered and followed. But your path won't take a miracle to find. You can uncover it by becoming a good destiny detective; that is, by taking a thoughtful look at your life story and inspecting some basic clues.

Here are five key questions to get your sleuthing underway:

1. Have you experienced serendipitous moments you knew amounted to something more than mere coincidence?

2. Do certain relationships seem to be leading "somewhere"? Do trusted friends, mentors, or family members encourage you in a specific pursuit or talent?

3. Are there particular activities that seem to make time fly and leave you feeling fulfilled?

4. Do you have a particular flair—a way of doing things— that causes others to solicit your help, advice, or expertise?

5. Is there something you dream of doing "someday"?

If more questions come to mind, pursue them. Take the time to excavate anecdotes and experiences you may have written off as happenstance. Read old journals; talk to family members. Study your resumé. You'll be surprised at the forgotten facts and memories that resurface.

Your sleuthing is not designed to rehash old news. You are looking for clues. In fact, you're looking for a system of information that has been demonstrated through your life experience. When viewed as a body of evidence, it will yield enormous insight, not only into your past, but also into your future.

What you are looking to uncover is what I call your *destiny code*. Everybody has one. Like everything else about you, your destiny code is one of a kind. Yes, even if you are an identical twin, your destiny code is unique. Once discovered, your destiny code will become a road map to your "Promised Land."

Like destiny itself, your destiny code encompasses every area of your life. It provides a big-picture view of what your fulfilled life will look like. It also includes many of the details that make you "you." Here's a working definition of *destiny code* from my book *Live Your Dream*:

> Your destiny code…is the system of symbols, signals, and patterns that you experience in your life, both in your thoughts and throughout your external circumstances. Included in your destiny code are your relationships and the providential connections that pave the way to your dreams. Your destiny code is woven into the fabric of your life and is reflected in the unique events which you have experienced. When you become aware of it, your destiny code will reveal your unique identity, purpose, and path. It is a detailed picture of your potential.[7]

Taken individually, these valuable clues could go unnoticed. As is common in detective work, the underlying truth of the story—in this case, your life story—becomes clear when the clues are taken together. Suddenly, the seemingly random threads winding through your history fall into place and form a discernible pattern. The pattern was there all along, but once you perceive it, you can extract its meaning and use the information it yields.

Your destiny code needn't remain a secret. It is, after all, *your* destiny code.

Making Meaning; Making a Difference

You'll remember that Viktor Frankl said, "Man's search for meaning is the primary motivation in his life…."[8] We also learned that, when the need for meaning is unmet, we feel empty, depressed, and frustrated. The need for meaning is a constant throughout our lives. It is not suspended in times of chaos or upheaval. Even when nothing around us seems to make sense, we maintain our role as meaning makers.

Viktor Frankl's extreme life experiences bear witness to this fact. In 1944, he was deported to a concentration camp. Upon their arrival at Auschwitz, Viktor and his wife, Tilly, were separated. Frankl was stripped of all but his eyeglasses, his shoes, and a belt. Also taken was a manuscript based on his life's work, the legacy he had hoped to leave the world.

Frankl and other new arrivals were ordered to select clothing from a pile of garments belonging to those already murdered at the camp.[9]

> Bereft of the book that was like his child, Viktor took a thin, torn coat from the heap. As he slipped his hand into one of the pockets, he felt the crinkle of a scrap of paper. He pulled it out and looked at it. It was a torn page from a Jewish prayer book. On it was written the Shema Yisrael, the prayer Viktor had seen and heard his father say every day when he was a boy: "Hear, O Israel, the Lord our God, the Lord is one God; and you shall love the Lord your God with all your heart and with all your soul and with all your strength." Viktor later wrote that finding this prayer in his "new" coat was a "challenge to me *to live* what I had written, to practice what I had preached." He kept that scrap of paper with him until he was liberated.[10]

In the midst of sheer brutality and seeming hopelessness, Viktor Frankl made meaning out of his circumstances. He found strength in words that were returned providentially to the front of his mind. Having lost all that he had known; having been forcibly separated from his beloved wife; and having lost the documentation of his life's work, Viktor found, in these words and through subsequent experiences, powerful reasons to survive the Holocaust.

> He had the realization while he was caught up on what he called "the endless little problems of our miserable life"—whether there would be sausage in the evening's rations, whether to exchange it for a piece of bread.... Suddenly, Viktor felt disgusted by his preoccupations. He began to daydream instead about standing on the platform of a warm, well-lit lecture hall. He saw himself lecturing about the psychology of the concentration camps. This dream became his goal, and ironically, focusing on that dream, rather than on survival, is what helped him survive.[11]

Making use of his time as a prisoner in several concentration camps, Frankl worked to bring hope to those who were distraught. After the liberation, he learned that Tilly had perished. He was devastated and considered suicide. Yet, because he was convinced of a greater purpose for his life, he rejected the thought of killing himself saying, "When all this happens to someone, to be tested in such a way…it must have some meaning. I have a feeling…that I am destined for something."[12]

Frankl was right. As a free man, he wrote and lectured about the psychology of the concentration camps and about the characteristics of those who managed to survive. He found meaning in the awful experience of the Holocaust by using it as a metaphor with which to bring others into wholeness.

Despite suffering catastrophic loss, Frankl fulfilled his destiny and became a difference-maker. He did so, in large part, because his need for meaning was met.

Your Calling Is Calling

Frankl's story is instructive in the extreme. Even so, it reveals that "following your bliss" is not always a tiptoe through the tulips. Unfolding destiny takes conscious participation and often, an uphill fight.

First, you must become aware that a previously hidden path—your path—has been exposed. But recognizing that path is only the beginning. To experience the unfolding of destiny, you must become consciously aware of the deeper meaning of your life and determined to connect with the very core of your identity (which is linked with that meaning).

This pursuit becomes increasingly directional as you tap into various aspects of your life's grand design. Instead of focusing on his plight in the camps, Frankl looked to the calling that was revealed to him there. He connected with who he was and what he was created to do. Because he was "making meaning," he no longer wrestled with self-concept, identity, and self-worth. He valued others and knew how to value himself. As he followed his calling, he accessed dimensions of his own psyche and spirit that had not previously been awakened. No longer preoccupied with confusion about identity, he was able to make room for these new inner dimensions.

Frankl emerged from the Holocaust well aware of his grand design. When we are similarly informed in the area of self-knowledge, we can discern our callings and pursue activities that are fulfilling and speak fully to the unique ways in which we were built. Absent this genuine knowledge of self, we engage in activities that drain rather than fulfill us. We become reliant upon others to define self-concept for us. Therefore, we become prone to performing for the sake of approval. Instead of doing the right thing, we do whatever other people say or seem to imply that we should do.

To be ready for the unfolding of destiny is to learn to live, not directed by others, but from the inside out. We are going to cover the gamut of ways in which inside-out living is accomplished; for now we can simply say that to live from the inside out is to live in a way that honestly expresses the person you were created to be. This includes knowing what it is that you want, need, and value.

The destiny-fulfilled life is a process of discovery. It means coming to a place where unfavorable circumstances, outright adversity, and imperfect relationships fail to limit you. Instead, you refuse to be defined or controlled by outside factors. You become motivated by the deeper meaning of your life and you pursue its fulfillment.

---

calling *noun*:

1. Vocation, profession, or trade.
2. A strong impulse or inclination.[13]

WHAT YOU WANT...WHAT YOU NEED

One of the most fundamental ways in which we make meaning is by being honest about our needs, wants, and values. We'll look closely at the subject of values in Chapter Three; first, let's take a look at productive ways to bring our needs and wants into sound alignment. This will help prepare us to apply the seven secrets effectively.

It is important to distinguish our wants from our needs. But why must we be able to tell them apart? For one thing, we want to remove any internal impediments to the successful unfolding of destiny. That is what Part I of this book is designed to do. One of the most common barriers to the outcome of overall fulfillment in life is the misunderstanding of what we really need and what we desire to have or experience.

"Confusing our wants with our needs gets us into trouble in the pursuit of purpose [or destiny]."[14] The trouble stems from the misplaced priorities and self-sabotaging behaviors that result from the confusion. We can see this in our own lives and in the lives of loved ones.

Consider this hypothetical example, which I think you will agree is both realistic and universal in its dynamics. A young woman, whom we will call *Elise*, attends medical school. Elise is always at the top of her class and works hard to stay there. She is seen as stellar among her classmates and the one most likely to blow off the party scene in order to ensure a strong academic performance.

Yet, Elise seems joyless in her pursuit when compared with her "less promising" classmates. Even Elise can see the excitement they exude in their shared dream of helping and healing others. Although she seems to be doing everything right, Elise approaches the "right" things she does as an end in themselves, rather than a means to a greater purpose. That is, until Elise is on the phone with her father, who is a prominent surgeon. The father loves Elise, but seems to favor her siblings, often in subliminal ways. When the two discuss her studies, Elise becomes animated; she excitedly reports her academic successes and inwardly hopes for her father's equally animated responses.

When her father's responses indicate approval, Elise is elated. Conversely, when her dad fails to meet the approval threshold Elise desires, she becomes downhearted and even more driven in her studies. By the time Elise begins her residency, she realizes that, although she has excelled on every academic and practical front, she is emotionally disconnected from her work. With each passing day, she becomes more disappointed with life.

Why would a successful student of medicine, for whom the future looks so bright and rewarding, feel empty in the pursuit of her noble profession? At least in part, the disconnect stems from the disparity between Elise's needs and wants. Remember that Elise perceives herself to be (and may well be) the least favored by her father, a man of prominence and considerable accomplishments. It could be for Elise, as it is for so many people, that what she *wants* is to become a doctor, while what she really *needs* (and has needed all along) is to be affirmed by her dad.

The need for parental affirmation is entirely legitimate, as we will see later. But when that need is unmet and a manufactured desire takes its place (as is true in Elise's life), the rest of life becomes dis-ordered. Misplaced priorities and skewed choices become unavoid-able, primarily because the motivation underlying all of it is unsound.

If Elise had recognized her genuine need, she could have addressed it in less damaging ways and would have been free to pursue a life based, not on her quest for love and affirmation, but on the fulfillment of her life's grand design.

Our choices in life are to be motivated by authentic meaning, not by unmet needs. When meaning is the driving force, we find that our needs and wants are met without frustration in healthy and reward-ing ways.

Checkpoint: Want or Need?

Can you relate to Elise? Is there any area in which your life parallels hers? Explain.

KNOW YOUR NEEDS

Our most obvious needs are biological; they are those elements and conditions that are vital for survival. We need air, water, food, and rest. We also need protection from the elements and from disease and injury. It has been shown that infants must experience human touch in order to survive. They must be sufficiently nurtured to survive and grow. Unless our biological needs are met, we will die.

We have other legitimate needs that have a significant impact on the outcomes we experience. Among these are the needs we experience at a spiritual or psychological level. Many of these needs are tied to your destiny code; they relate to whom you were created to be, what you were created to do, and what you were created to have. These needs fall into four main categories:

1. Career/calling

2. Family life

3. Relational/social life

4. Financial life

These needs are not superficial. However, they can become distorted if we attempt to meet them for the wrong reasons and by counterfeit means. This is what happened in the case of Elise, whose career path had been decided, not by her true calling, but in an ill-conceived attempt to fulfill a relational deficiency.

VET YOUR WANTS

Like needs, the legitimacy of our wants is based on the motivation underlying our pursuits. By definition, our wants don't meet the threshold of being necessary for survival. Our desires, when accurately distinguished from our needs, are not survival-related at all. Instead, they are life enhancements; we seek them to improve the quality of our lives.

Many of our wants are sound and motivated by legitimate priorities. For example, if you are married and have one child, you and your family could manage in a one-bedroom apartment. Families around the world survive with much less. Yet you probably prefer a separate bedroom for your child. This is not an extravagant preference; it provides a sound arrangement for rest and privacy. Yet, it still qualifies as an enhancement—an addition that makes life better. Neither you, your spouse, nor your baby would perish for lack of a second bedroom.

The key to managing our wants and prioritizing them accurately is to recognize them for what they are. When we mistake a desire—for a certain car, a particular home, a child with a certain personality—for a *need*, we fail to appreciate what we already have. Because our priorities are out of order, our expectations become skewed. We suffer endless cycles of frustration because nothing seems to satisfy. In our striving for the things we want, we unwittingly deprioritize genuine needs such as rest, intimacy, and authenticity. Frustration increases, and life grows emptier each day.

But when you are motivated by what is meaningful, you become clear-eyed. You assess the condition of your life accurately. You recognize your blessings and you proactively address any shortfalls. You see each day as a brand-new opportunity to advance. Perhaps best of all, with meaning as your motivation, you gain access to the resources you need to experience your unfolding destiny.

NEEDS AND WANTS CONTRASTED	
Needs	Wants
I need to pursue a career that fulfills my calling in life and provides for my family's needs.	I'm looking for a position that projects the social and financial status I deserve.
As a spouse, I need to both foster and enjoy a relationship based on mutual love and respect.	It is important for my marriage to be seen by others as being happy.
I seek to have the right friends for the right reasons—those to whom I am called and who are called to be in relationship with me.	It is important to me to have many friends who are supportive of my choices and are there when I need them.
I seek a sound financial life that is balanced with a sound spiritual, social, and family life.	I have certain monetary goals in mind and will work ceaselessly to reach them. I know my family will benefit in the long run, regardless of the relational cost now.

Figure 2

ENDNOTES

1. "World of Computer Science on Alan C. Kay," Book Rags, http://www.bookrags.com/biography/alan-c-kay-wcs/ (accessed August 27, 2009).

2. "Destiny," Merriam-Webster Online Dictionary (2009), Merriam-Webster Online, http://www.merriam-webster.com/dictionary/destiny (accessed October 28, 2009).

3. Scott Gasch, "Alan Kay" (biography submitted in partial fulfillment of CS3604 course requirements related to Virginia Tech/Norfolk State University project "Interactive Learning with a Digital Library in Computer Science" program, Fall 1996, copyright 1996, 2005), http://ei.cs.vt.edu/~history/GASCH.KAY.HTML.

4. "Unfold," Dictionary.com, Dictionary.com Unabridged, v. 1.1 (Random House, Inc.), http://dictionary.reference.com/browse/unfold (accessed July 02, 2009).

5. "Foreordain," Dictionary.com, Dictionary.com Unabridged, v. 1.1 (Random House, Inc.), http://dictionary.reference.com/browse/foreordain (accessed July 02, 2009).

6. "The Power of Myth," Joseph Campbell Foundation (transcript with Bill Moyers), 113, 120, http://www.jcf.org/new/index.php?categoryid=31 (accessed June 23, 2009).

7. Dr. Mark Chironna, *Live Your Dream*, (Shippensburg, PA: Destiny Image, 2009), 28.

8. Viktor Frankl, *Man's Search for Meaning* (Boston: Beacon Press, 1992), 105, http://books.google.com/books?id=K2AvZmco3E0C&dq=man's+search+for+meaning+victor+frankl&printsec=frontcover&source=bl&ots=cKnkG1CAgh&sig=EWojeCGMMlXdMUeOoppa8ajTUfY&hl=en&ei=uEFBSrOoH4j2sQPW8tDxCA&sa=X&oi=book_result&ct=result&resnum=5 (accessed July 2, 2009).

9. Anna Redsand, *Viktor Frankl: A Life Worth Living* (New York: Clarion Books, 2006), 70.

10. Ibid.

11. Ibid., 75.

12. Ibid., 86.

13. "Calling," Dictionary.com, Dictionary.com Unabridged, v. 1.1 (Random House, Inc.), http://dictionary.reference.com/browse/calling (accessed July 02, 2009).

14. Dr. Mark Chironna, *Stepping Into Greatness* (Lake Mary, FL: Charisma House, 1999), 125.

UNFOLD YOUR DESTINY

1. Think about your most life-changing experience to date. In what ways did this experience uncover a deeper meaning in your life? How has that revelation affected your attitudes and conduct?

2. What do you consider to be your five most essential needs? Which of these needs are being met, and how? Which do you consider to be unmet?

3. What are your five greatest desires? How do they differ from your needs?

CHAPTER THREE

Values at Your Core

"Education without values, as useful as it is,
seems rather to make man a more clever devil."
—C.S. Lewis

E VERY DAY, WE FACE choices. Close the big overseas deal or attend your daughter's kindergarten graduation? Tell a loved one the difficult truth that could avert a downfall or curry favor by holding your peace?

You don't need me to tell you that life has its quandaries. The tough choices we face are among them. But even daunting choices needn't be complicated. No matter the relational challenges, choices are simplified when you know what your guiding principles are. As is true of your needs and wants, understanding your deeply held values can bring clarity to the conduct of your life and keep you on the path of your unfolding destiny.

The *value* of something is its "relative worth, merit, or importance...import or meaning...significance...."[1] When you value something, you are mindful of its worth; you recognize its meaning; you acknowledge its significance; you care for it well; you guard and even treasure it; you take whatever steps are necessary to ensure its continued value.

We claim to value many things: our loved ones, our homes, the faith that guides us, our jobs and professions, education, honesty, compassion, and yes, money. How we prioritize that which we hold dear paints a picture of who we really are. It says something about how we are built and about how committed we are to what we believe. Our priorities reveal our values.

So what are values? In a sociological sense, our values can be described as "the ideals, customs, institutions, etc., of a society toward which the people of the group have an affective regard. These values may be positive, as cleanliness, freedom, or education, or negative, as cruelty, or blasphemy."[2]

But what are values on a personal level, and why are they so important? Let's start with a simple working definition:

Your values are the things that matter most in your life. They are based on the things you believe most deeply and hold to be true.

Values are important because they become the standards by which we live, govern, and evaluate our lives. Our values affect our thoughts, actions, attitudes, opinions, and choices. They color our relationships and even our dispositions. Our values play a role in the workplace, in our hobbies, and ultimately in the unfolding of our life stories. Our values are somewhat fluid; many of the values we hold as adults differ from those we had as children.

Values affect our outcomes. When we engage in pursuits and activities that are congruent with our values, we are less likely to experience distress, struggle, resistance, and conflict. We experience the ease that comes with being at peace with our choices. We have a sense of being in the flow that leads us where we want to go, not because destiny fulfillment is the easiest path, but because we are not torn, tortured by inner conflict, or divided within ourselves.

When you enter this kind of values-aligned ease in one area of your life, you tend to experience the same ease in other activities and endeavors. When your values become the ultimate arbiters of your priorities, you make choices that benefit your life across all platforms. It's as though the pieces begin falling into place to build a well-oiled machine—one that can transport you smoothly from Point A to Point B.

DISCOVER AND AFFIRM YOUR VALUES

We have touched briefly on definitions of personal values and values in the broader societal sense. Although almost all people and peoples hold certain values in common, they do vary somewhat from nation to nation. In the United States of America, some of our most fundamental values are stated in The Declaration of Independence:

...We hold these truths to be self-evident, that all men are created equal, that they are endowed by their Creator with certain unalienable Rights, that among

these are Life, Liberty and the pursuit of Happiness.—
That to secure these rights, Governments are instituted
among Men, deriving their just powers from the consent
of the governed....[3]

The Founding Fathers perceived the need to state in clear
terms the fundamental values that compelled the formation of our
nation. These values were then affirmed in the U.S. Constitution.
They guide our nation's conduct even today. First and foremost
among these original values is the idea that all people are created
equal. This was not a value held by all governments in the eighteenth century; nor is it considered a self-evident truth in many
countries today.

We can summarize the values expressed in our excerpt from
The Declaration of Independence as follows:

- All people are created equal.

- They are endowed with rights that cannot be repudi-
  ated; these include life, liberty, and the pursuit of
  happiness.

- These rights are endowed, not by government, but
  by the Creator.

- Government derives its power, not from its own
  existence, but from the consent of the people.

As you consider these stated national values, it is easy to
understand how monumental they are when applied or withheld.
Their importance cannot be overstated. Therefore, it is important
for each of us to be familiar with the tenets that give our nation
meaning. Absent a shared knowledge and appreciation of them,
lawlessness prevails and unity is threatened.

The same is true on an individual level. We know that congruence between one's values and pursuits yields a certain ease in life, while a lack of congruence promotes struggle, resistance, and conflict. But what happens when our values are unclear? The answer is: *confusion.* Without the guidance of clear values, we are adrift. We stumble through one decision after another, haphazardly throwing the disordered threads of our lives against the wall like wet strands of spaghetti that we hope will stick.

Thankfully, a completely valueless life is nearly impossible to achieve. In fact, there are some values so common to all peoples as to be inherent in our humanness.

These *core values* prepare us for unfolding destiny.

DIG DEEP—TO YOUR CORE

Although each human being is a unique creation, we share certain basic needs, wants, and values. It is true for all that our biological needs must be met in order for us to survive. All of us desire opportunity and sound relationships; we protect these areas of our lives because we deem them to have value or significance. These shared characteristics add meaning to our individual roles and to our individual aspirations.

Among these characteristics are our *core values.* Author, preeminent executive life coach, and founder of *The Hudson Institute,* Frederic M. Hudson isolated six of these values after having "examined 250 biographies of successful adults…[and] searching for the dominant inner anchors that guided people toward realizing their own greatness."[4]

We will focus on Hudson's six core values, as described in his landmark work, *The Handbook of Coaching.* There are more than six core values; typically, researchers list between 25 and 30 for adults. The significance of the six values Hudson isolated is found in the lives he selected for study over the course of 20 years. Hudson studied those people who experienced unfolding destiny. He found that each of them displayed six core values in a variety of combinations.

Of these abiding core values, there is no set combination that applies to everyone or that applies at every stage of life. Every individual experiences an ebb and flow of values through life's many seasons. At any given time, three core values will tend to be predominant; but the order of predominance varies over time. And, just as values change after childhood, they also shift as we move through each decade of adult life.

YOUR "DEEP" SIX CORE VALUES

Before we cover in depth the six core values from Hudson's studies, here's a brief summary and description of the values as listed by Hudson:

HUDSON'S SIX CORE VALUES[5]
1. Personal identity/power: Claiming yourself
2. Achievement: Proving yourself
3. Intimacy: Sharing yourself
4. Play and creativity: Expressing yourself
5. Search for meaning: Integrating yourself
6. Compassion and contribution: Giving yourself

Figure 3

As we dig deeper, consider the presence and function of these values in your own life. Pause to explore any questions that arise in your mind or write them down for future consideration. Don't let them slip by; they are precious opportunities to gain insight about yourself and the conduct of your life—now and in the future. Do the same with any personal anecdotes, observations, or revelations that are triggered in your memory; they are potentially powerful tools of learning and destiny advancement!

PERSONAL IDENTITY[6]

As you can see in Figure 3, Hudson subtitles this value "claiming yourself." This core value involves your view of self; it is the picture that describes who you are at the most fundamental, yet potentially monumental level.

You claim yourself by asking the tough questions about who you are and why you're here. To explore your sense of identity and purpose is an act of personal power. It means taking ownership of your life and learning where you are headed. It implies a certain level of self-knowledge, self-awareness, and spiritual awareness. It acknowledges your magnificent intricacies, the facets that are uniquely combined to make you "you."

The core value of personal identity focuses on who you are apart from everyone else. Yet elements of it hint at your interconnectedness with others, especially in regard to personal boundaries. Your personal boundaries speak to the space in this world that you perceive yourself to occupy, emotionally and otherwise. They define your sense of how much space is yours—where you end and others begin, so to speak.

Personal identity also deals with elements such as self-esteem, self-reliance, self-responsible behavior, and self-confidence, all of which affect personal performance, the quality of your relationships, and personal development over the course of your life.

As a core value, personal identity operates differently at different ages. From the time you are born until somewhere in mid-life, personal identity involves self-discovery and learning to be empowered from the inside out (not driven by externals, but by internals such as your calling, purpose, and destiny codes). In the second half of life, personal identity becomes more centered on the inner connection to your life's purpose and the desire to be linked with something "bigger" than you.

Remember that every core value evolves over your lifetime and occupies a different level of predominance as your needs change. Apart from these seasonal fluctuations, every individual has personal strengths and weaknesses. Some of our core values are better defined than others. When we probe our values, we trigger new opportunities to develop them more fully and to reap the rewards of the guidance they provide.

Having a clear sense of personal identity is a formidable source of personal power that frees you to live authentically, from the inside out. We'll tackle these aspects of empowerment and authenticity more fully in coming chapters. For now, enjoy this personal identity "appetizer" and dig deeper with the following questions.

Core Checkpoint 1

1. How highly do you esteem yourself, and what factors have affected your sense of self-esteem?

2. How comfortable are you with self-reliance? What aspects of your life reflect your comfort level?

3. Where are your personal boundaries? Are they based in a healthy sense of identity, or are they a self-protection mechanism used to manage fear and intimidation?

ACHIEVEMENT

While the first core value has to do with your sense of *being*, achievement has to do with your *doing*. It is the hub of the wheel whose spokes include the compelling pursuits of purpose and legacy. This value ensures that your ambitions and activities remain wired to the same circuit as your dominant need, which directly involves your calling and the achievement of results related to that calling.

Because achievement involves what you do, it must also encompass your effectiveness and preparedness. It includes an accounting of the presence, development, and application of your gifts and talents.

For example, if you are called to be a concert pianist, you will seek to perform at a high level. Your destiny fulfillment will require a commitment to excellence far above that of the "average" musician. Your knowledge of music theory, composers, technique, and performance will need to be extensive and ever-expanding. Those who can provide opportunities to audition, perform, and compete will expect you to be in top form at all times—and at a moment's notice.

Your choices and activities will need to reflect your ambitions. Your success as a concert pianist will demand an honest and ongoing examination of your skill set, as well as a commitment to continued training. When you embrace the core value of achievement, you will be open to the constructive criticism of an accomplished mentor. Your desire to fulfill your calling will promote introspection and growth. It will also cause you to reach a level of personal development at which you will be able to lead others. Guided by this core value, your pursuit will be marked by intentionality and the formation of a strategic life plan that will enable you to leave your mark on the world.

Just as a strong sense of personal identity is necessary for destiny-fulfillment, a clear understanding of your purpose and of the rewards you seek will empower you to conduct your life in ways that support the unfolding of your destiny.

Pragmatic, purpose-driven issues such as goal attainment, the conduct of specific projects, effective methods, and the achievement of milestones (signs of victory)—all of these fall under the purview of Hudson's second core value.

These elements are often more easily measured than the elements of personal identity. This measurability makes them useful in providing a sense of "location"; it helps you to assess which goals and rewards have already been attained and which are yet to be pursued and accomplished.

In regard to goal attainment and strategic life planning,[7] your assessment should include plans for secondary goals to be pursued once your original goals are attained. These new goals would also be tied to your life's purpose, but would be designed from the perspective of your continued personal development. Good goal-setting means tailoring and adjusting your goals to meet the evolving needs of each life season and the evolving needs of society at large.

Core Checkpoint 2

1. Toward which of your goals are you progressing steadily? Which goals seem to be stalled?

2. Are you adequately prepared to achieve your goals? What steps can you take to improve your preparation and win at what you do?

3. When your current goals are met, which goals are next?

INTIMACY

Intimacy involves sharing yourself with others. The word is used here in the broader sense and goes beyond physical intimacy. It involves developing the ability to love yourself even while allowing others into your life. It also involves the extent to which you know yourself and allow others to know you. This core value examines your willingness to invest in yourself and in others. As a value, intimacy helps you to evaluate the overall health of your relationships and of the love that flows through them.

You cannot share what you do not possess: the ability to love others begins with a sound love of self. When you love yourself, you are more willing to accept the primary risk of intimacy: the vulnerability to emotional hurt. Instead of fearing loss, you become interested in what kind of friend you are and how you can be a better one. No longer do you need to be the center of the transaction, but a participant in the give and take of bonding, caring, nurturing, and all the other building blocks of intimate relationships.

Intimacy can be a one-on-one dynamic, but the core value of intimacy encompasses intimacy in the sense of family, too. Therefore, it values the process of nesting, coupling, and parenting so that children can experience the bonding, caring, and nurturing that will prepare them for intimacy in their adult lives.

Core Checkpoint 3

1. How successful are you at maintaining a healthy sense of self-love while entering into loving relationships with others?

2. Are you a passive or proactive player in your relationships? Do you actively engage in the give and take of loving, bonding, caring, and nurturing, or do you wait for others to initiate?

3. To what degree do you allow yourself to be known? Do your relational boundaries promote healthy intimacy or overprotect you and conceal your authentic identity?

PLAY AND CREATIVITY

You've heard the adage, "All work and no play makes Johnny a dull boy." Truer words could not be spoken. We are complex beings designed to live multi-faceted lives that stimulate and refresh, motivate and restore. Without the natural ebb and flow between programs and spontaneity…work and play…inside- and outside-the-box living, our lives become one-dimensional, self-focused, and physically depleting.

The core value of play and creativity makes room for the precious but non-purposeful moments in life. These are the very moments in which we are regenerated, soul and body. Often, we call this quality time, the time we spend alone or with others exploring the lighter, more personal side of life. Whether your sense of play and creativity is fulfilled by watching cartoons, playing board games with friends, telling jokes, or writing poetry, you are expressing yourself, perhaps in your most unguarded and least structured manner.

Play and creativity involve activities that release the freedom to be imaginative, unscripted, celebratory, funny, original, joyful, and playful. Because this freedom suspends expectations of productivity, perfection, and reward, it often leads to unexpected encounters with artistry and innovation—the "aha" moments described in the biographies of great inventors and pioneers.

Play and creativity help you to clear your mind and reset emotionally. Times of refreshment and repair groom you for renewed passion in your purpose-driven pursuits, making you far more productive in the long-term than you would have been had you never stepped back from the more serious side of life.

Core Checkpoint 4

1. When was the last time you had a good belly-laugh with a friend or loved one? What were you doing at the time and how did the moment affect you?

2. How often do you allow yourself to think about something other than the serious matters in your life? Have you given yourself permission to apply your imagination to the lighter side of life?

3. Are you willing to risk being silly or playful? If not, what unspoken standard (or value judgment) is preventing you from doing so?

SEARCH FOR MEANING

We've talked about the human drive to find meaning; we'll discuss this need in various contexts in coming chapters. Frederic Hudson found in his studies that, for those who experience the unfolding of destiny, the search for meaning is a core value. That is not surprising, since meaning determines purpose.

Do you remember what Viktor Frankl said about meaning? He said it is the primary motivation in our lives.[8] This motivation is intertwined with our spirituality as human beings. We are interested in more than conversations about the weather; we have an inherent need to understand deeper truths about ourselves and what we are doing here. We want to identify what Hudson calls our "ultimate concern."[9] We want to identify our beliefs and our callings. All of these questions of meaning are an effort to connect us with something bigger than anything we can touch, explain, or imagine.

The search for meaning involves not only our spirituality but our integrity. This integrity is foundational. It is not so much about your word being good as it is about the reasons why you say what you mean and can be trusted to follow through on it. It has to do with the full integration of your interior life—a spiritual, emotional, and cognitive orderliness; a genuine state of peace that stems from a sense of being reconciled in your ultimate concern; a contemplative approach to life that seeks to think both on the big picture and the glorious details of life; a sense of transcendence in which you are free from enemies within, and delivered from slavery to unimportant things.

This core value is present throughout your lifetime, but in times of transition, it comes to the forefront as a vital thread connecting the season that is ending with the one that is just beginning. The search for meaning creates a stabilizing sense of continuity that helps you to bridge the chasm between the known past and the unknown period ahead.

Because the search for meaning is an ever-present human need, to ignore it early is to invite unnecessary crises later. For example, the 30-something professional or homemaker or construction worker who fails to make meaning out of life's competing interests—career, family, spirituality, emotional needs—and instead keeps plugging away in the belief that he or she will sort it out someday, is apt to experience a rude awakening in the form of a midlife crisis of one kind or another. Because the crisis was years in the making, it could be difficult to detangle and damaging to long-term relationships and concerns.

Core Checkpoint 5

1. Are there key areas of your life that seem to be continually relegated to the back burner? How can you better integrate these from the inside out?

2. How attentive have you been to addressing and resolving your need for meaning, particularly in regard to issues of ultimate concern?

3. In what ways does your life express the integrity that demonstrates a sense of orderly alignment within yourself? Do your actions comport with the greater meaning of your life? Do your outcomes reflect your dreams? Explain.

COMPASSION AND CONTRIBUTION

You'll remember that the second core value was achievement, of which a key element was the pursuit of legacy. Hudson's sixth core value deals not only with legacy-building, but with the leaving behind of a legacy to nourish others.

From the standpoint of core values, compassion and contribution tend to become more predominant during midlife. This is the time in life when you realize that the years which live in your memories are greater in number than those that are ahead. Suddenly, you become aware of just how short life is. You become more concerned with having something to give others, something that will outlive you, yet express your concern for other people, for the community, for political or social issues, or for the less fortunate.

This is when you look outside yourself and your own needs to identify the causes you choose to support and the ways in which you want to volunteer your time and services. The drive is dual: to express your compassion and to give to others—whether through mentoring, caring, leading, reforming, supporting, or helping in whatever ways you believe you can be effective.

Core Checkpoint 6

Has this core value shifted to the forefront in your life or in the life of a loved one? Explain how.

VALUES KEYS

Because your core values are so integrally involved in the conduct of your life, any disconnection between your values and your needs and wants will bring unnecessary confusion, distress, and discomfort. When you feel out of kilter over an issue or situation, check your alignment!

Another key is to avoid locking yourself into your current configuration of core values. Remember that your life is composed of many seasons during which your needs change. In addition, the cavalcade of changing circumstances that you experience over time will lead you into ever-evolving searches for meaning. Each will lead you somewhere new, a place from which you will need to draw upon a new combination of values.

The fullest expression of unfolding destiny is never about having arrived, but about living in a state of conscious awareness and active engagement even as things change.

It's about sticking with the journey and riding on!

ENDNOTES

1. "Value," Dictionary.com, Dictionary.com Unabridged, v. 1.1 (Random House, Inc.), http://dictionary.reference.com/browse/value (accessed July 07, 2009).

2. Ibid.

3. "The Declaration of Independence," The National Archives, Archives. gov, http://www.archives.gov/exhibits/charters/declaration_transcript.html (accessed July 7, 2009).

4. Frederic M. Hudson, Ph.D., *The Handbook of Coaching*, 1st ed., (New York: Jossey-Bass, 1999), 127.

5. Ibid., 127-128.

6. All discussion of the Six Core Values includes concepts from: Frederic M. Hudson, Ph.D., *The Handbook of Coaching*, 1st ed. (New York: Jossey-Bass, 1999), 127-130.

7. For details on developing your strategic life plan, see my book, *Live Your Dream* (Shippensburg, PA: Destiny Image, 2009).

8. Viktor Frankl, *Man's Search for Meaning* (Boston: Beacon Press, 1992), 105, http://books.google .com/books?id=K2AvZmco3E0C&dq=man's+search+for+meaning+victor+frankl&printsec=frontcover&source=bl&ots=cKnkG1CAgh&sig=EWojeCGMMlXdMUeOoppa8ajTUfY&hl=en&ei=uEFBSrOoH4j2sQP

W8tDxCA&sa=X&oi=book_result&ct=result&resnu m=5 (accessed July 7, 2009).

9. Hudson, *Handbook of Coaching*, 130.

Unfold Your Destiny

Imagine that you have everything you ever need or want the very moment the need or want becomes apparent. Would this unusual condition affect adherence to your core values? Would the effect be positive, negative, or neutral? Explain.

CHAPTER FOUR

Living From
the Inside Out

*"I don't want to get to the end of my life and
find that I have lived just the length of it.
I want to have lived the width of it as well."*
—Diane Ackerman

CERTAIN TASKS IN LIFE ARE linear. You buy your child a toy that requires assembly. You line up the pieces on the living room floor, unfurl the instructions, and begin to read:

Step 1. Align the screw hole in the thingamabob with the screw hole in the whatchamacallit.

Step 2. Insert screw.

Step 3. Turn the screw....

Step 93. Save the leftover screws (you just might need them).

The unfolding of life is anything but linear. You cannot measure its length, breadth, height, or depth by conventional means. Life is layered. It is multi-dimensional. Its colors change; its sounds evolve. Life has almost infinite potential for richness, texture, complexity, satisfaction, delight. In the larger scheme of things, it is a wonderland of opportunity, a vast field of open doorways into your next adventure.

Although much of life plays out in externals (events, circumstances, wins, losses, etc.), much more of life happens on the inside. Your thoughts, the search for meaning, your inner calling, your destiny codes—they help form a pathway to destiny that leads from the inside out. This path ultimately affects everyone around you and creates a legacy to leave to those who come after you.

LIFE'S TOTAL PACKAGE

In Chapter Two, I mentioned that your destiny encompasses every area of your life from the inside out. There are seven major areas with which most of us identify:

1. Your spiritual life—this includes your religious beliefs; the role of faith in your life; the belief that your life is not just about you, but has a larger meaning.

2. Your vocational life—this speaks to your work; professional aspirations; career track; intellectual life; and

educational endeavors, including the training and mentoring which help equip you.

3. Your psychological life—included are your mental state, including cognitive function and emotional conduct; your patterns of thought; your moods and predispositions; and the combined effect of these on the whole of your life.

4. Your family life—this includes your interaction and role in the family unit, your sense of family heritage, your commitment to loved ones, your capacity for intimacy, and your ability to integrate family concerns with the rest of your life.

5. Your social life—this area covers the broad spectrum of your relational life and non-professional activities. It includes quality time spent with friends, dating and courting, recreation, your interaction with coworkers, and your involvement in social circles and organizations.

6. Your physical life—this includes the value you place on the well-being of your physical body; your involvement in physical activities, including sex; your lifestyle choices, including dietary and conditioning choices; and your overall physical capacity and condition.

7. Your financial life—this includes your perspectives about money, including any financial fears, chronic overspending, or hoarding tendencies; your earning power; your money management and financial planning; your approach to marital finances; your financial priorities; your charitable donations; and your beliefs about tithing, taxes, and saving.

Just as we know that certain values come to the forefront at different stages of our lives, so different areas of life come to the forefront in various seasons. A well-integrated life embraces all seven areas in varying concentrations as our changing needs demand.

EMPOWERMENT IS AN "INSIDE JOB"

Over the course of your life, it is likely that you have been empowered by others—parents, teachers, your spouse—at one point or another. Your parents may have taught you to be persistent, honest, and proactive. A particular teacher may have affirmed a particular gift and encouraged you to develop it. Your spouse may have supported a certain endeavor by offering to help or to lighten your load at home.

To be empowered in these ways is to be assisted along your destiny path. However, your destiny path exists regardless of the degree to which others support or cooperate with it. In the final analysis, your empowerment has more to do with you than it does them.

Empowerment is an inside job. You are empowered when your inner values and core criteria are connected with the outer dreams, goals, objectives, and outcomes for which you long and were created to obtain. You already know what values, goals, dreams, and objectives are. (We will further explore outcomes later in this chapter.) But what are your *core criteria?*

Very briefly, your core criteria are the desire, intent, and passion related to your dream. Assuming you have consciously explored and implemented the keys we have discussed so far, your *desires* are aligned with your purpose and your values because they are destiny desires. Therefore, they inspire rather than cause distress. (The key is to become consciously aware of your desires and make sure they are not "borrowed" from someone you wish to emulate or imposed by someone you seek to please.)

Your *intent* is "the conscious direction of your efforts toward a specific goal or objective."[1] It is the difference between simply wanting something and making a commitment to obtain or achieve it. Intent will help you to leap the hurdles and stay on course when discouragement or difficulties obstruct your path.

Your passions are seen in the pursuits and activities that cause you to come alive. They exhilarate, stir you to action, and reveal what makes you tick. Whether it's politics or humanitarian causes, songwriting or accounting, your passions are clues to your destiny code.

THE CONSCIOUS, EMPOWERED LIFE

When you connect your inner values and core criteria with the things you are seeking "out there," you are empowered to live fully, deeply, and in harmony with your destiny. This is a conscious state of being; in fact, to be empowered is to live fully conscious of these elements and of all the aspects of unfolding destiny.

Imagine this scenario: Your life's dream is to teach middle-school students. It is clear from your history that your core criteria are in alignment with your dream: You have desired to enter this profession for as long as you can remember. You are passionate about the development and success of young people. There is no doubt about your intent to serve them: you have excelled in your own education and have jumped through the hoops necessary to achieve your certification.

Your core values are also lining up: identity, achievement, intimacy, play and creativity, search for meaning, compassion and contribution—all are working together in the classroom and even in your prep time to yield the fruit that is produced by those who live in harmony with their destinies. You have an ease about your interaction and are having a positive impact on the young people entrusted to you. They love being in your class; they excel in the subjects you teach; those who once lacked confidence are becoming self-assured. As your students prosper in their studies, you are reaping the benefits of destiny fulfillment. You are inspired and joyful and becoming more innovative as the years go on. Your awareness is heightened and you feel fully alive.

You are *empowered.*

What is the opposite of empowerment? It is to live on auto-pilot, driven by the unconscious mind and succumbing to the thoughts, tendencies, and attitudes that operate in the background of mental and emotional function.

Consider a second scenario: Your core criteria are lined up just as they were in the first example. But now, the ease in your interaction is lacking. An unconscious fear of rejection is preventing you from being authentic in the classroom. You are guarded. Instead of excelling, you are going through the motions, afraid to share yourself with your students. You shrink back from the core value of intimacy because you feel vulnerable to emotional hurt. You worry that this roomful of pre-teens will see right through you. At some level, you fear they will judge or ridicule you. You worry that, if they do, your career will be over. So you self-protect: instead of engaging your students, you unwittingly create a forbidding gulf that stifles genuine interaction and hinders learning. All the while, you are on auto-pilot, unaware of the real cause of the breakdown in your classroom.

In part because we are unaware of the activity of these unconscious "programs," they are free to control us by default. They undermine our best efforts or abort them altogether. They keep us subliminally preoccupied with all that is counter-productive: our insecurities, sense of inadequacy, and other fear-based perspectives. They blind us to the reasons for our behaviors. These defaults blind us to life's larger picture and bind us to misalignment and unfavorable outcomes.

Thankfully, we can choose to live the fully conscious life. (Part I of this book is devoted to that very cause!) The more we learn about ourselves (warts and all), the better we understand our purpose. The sooner we embrace the promise of conscious destiny-fulfillment, the more empowered we become.

Empowerment Checkpoint

To what degree do you feel empowered from the inside out? To what degree do you look to others to empower you?

YOUR LIFE STORY

At any given moment, you are the sum total of every thought you have ever had, every word you have ever spoken, every emotion you have ever felt, and every deed you have ever done. Who you are today is entwined with your life story to this point.

Your life story is unique; it cannot be duplicated. Neither can it be undone; the parts of your life story that are already written are history. If you are living your dreams, thrilled with your work, blessed in your family life, and flying high financially, you are probably OK with the idea that your life story cannot be erased. But, if life has not worked out as you had hoped, if you are regretting your choices or feeling stuck in a rut, the thought of an indelible life story might sound like bad news.

It's not. You are still breathing; therefore, the current version of your life story is not the final draft. You still have unlimited room for growth. But understand this: your maximum growth potential isn't realized when you ignore or deny your life story; it is realized when you *own* it.

How do you own your life story? You start by acknowledging life's failures and disappointments. Anyone who has taken ownership of his life story has done so by facing down the ghosts of the past. You can't own something you refuse to look at. Instead, you have to examine it; acknowledge its condition; and dig under the decay to find the meaning, the purpose, and the value in it.

You do this by asking the hard questions:

- What can I take from this experience?

- Which negative tendencies keep cropping up and what do they tell me?

- Which thought patterns, traits, and tendencies do I need to carry forward and which do I need to leave behind?

Once you have faced the truth squarely, you can release your life story from the death grip of regret and move forward without the baggage of so much old news. This is empowerment as it relates to what has come before. It is only after you have asked yourself the hard questions that you are ready for destiny fulfillment. Let's face it; your life story has had a profound impact on where you are today. There's no getting around that fact. You can drag it around under layers of disguise, blame, and self-hatred or you can own it, let it go, and move on.

When you own your life story in this way, you are choosing a path of grace—acknowledging the ups and downs and rights and wrongs, and accepting them as a part of life. This taking of ownership establishes your life story as belonging to something larger and more contextual—your personal history, a testimony to your life in all its fullness and fluidity. In the volume of your personal history, every page, however painful it may be, is meaningful.

When you take ownership of your life story, you validate it on the basis of your inherent worth as a human being. It becomes a statement of your commitment, an affirmation that you are empowered. When your life story becomes part of your personal history, "it becomes a powerful force of motivation to propel you into greater levels of your destiny."[2]

COMPREHEND YOUR PERSONAL HISTORY

Your personal history is composed of certain constants that remain even as the seasons of your life shift. These continuing aspects of life operate in uninterrupted connection, sequence, and succession throughout the years. Much like the core values that are present in varying combinations over the course of your lifetime, these constants—whatever their sequence or emphases—remain interconnected. They are present in your earliest memories; they have always been there regardless of your circumstances.

These enduring characteristics provide a sense of strong connection, both to your past and your future. They support a life that is grounded. They produce an element of safety, a confidence that no matter what happens, you will land on your feet. For example, if you were raised in a large, loving family, you can remember always having loved ones around when you needed them most. You trust in the fact that, even as you grow into adulthood, your loved ones will see you through life's ups and downs. As the years progress, you might raise a family of your own, expanding this base of support and interaction. Even as the elders of the family pass off the scene, the constant of family support remains.

Some of your personal history is more fluid: certain relationships come and go; locations change; belief systems evolve; losses occur; gains are made; some pursuits run their course and new ones begin. These changes are part of life's transitions from one season to the next. Diapers, dollhouses, homes, and job descriptions—all are subject to change in the normal course of maturation.

Your exit from the womb was the first of many transitions; your reaction was to cry vehemently. Transition isn't always pleasant; but even when change seems unfavorable or outright unwanted, it opens doors to new structures and possibilities. These new structures may be internal; they may be positive changes in your belief system that give way to fresh perceptions. Or, they may be new fields of opportunity (or even a new awareness of already existing opportunities).

Fluidity is the very nature of these shifts. New dynamics accompany transitions. They launch us out of lethargy and enlarge our capacities. We begin to rethink old ideas or discard them altogether; we increase our emotional endurance and become more persevering; we reevaluate our risk aversion and unwillingness to live outside the box.

The fear of change typically rears its head during times of transition. This fear has affected human beings throughout history. Listen to what D.H. Lawrence says about the human response to change:

The world fears a new experience more than it fears anything. Because a new experience displaces so many old experiences. And it is like trying to use muscles that have perhaps never been used, or that have been going stiff for ages. It hurts horribly.

The world doesn't fear a new idea. It can pigeon-hole any idea. But it can't pigeon-hole a real new experience. It can only dodge.[3]

History records our distrust of new experiences. In part, this resistance stems from our unending search for meaning. In the early days of the Christian Church, at a large public gathering on the Day of Pentecost, people began to speak in languages they did not know. Others recognized the sound of their native tongues being spoken by these "foreigners" and were baffled. Some attributed the strange occurrence to drunkenness. This dismissive approach is not surprising. This was a new experience that could not be explained by natural means; it naturally drew skepticism. Once the experience was explained to the satisfaction of the crowd, thousands readily embraced it.[4] Yet, not everyone did.

New experiences challenge our paradigms and often breach the bastions of resistance. They open our vision to new vistas that are integral to the process of unfolding destiny.

CHANGING SEASONS

No matter who you are, your life is marked by seasons. Some seasons are joyous, fun, and invigorating. Others try the soul, drain vitality, and leave you questioning the meaning of life. No matter the season or what it brings, it has the power to create new "sparks" and release unseen potential. These sparks are essential to unfolding destiny.

Some seasons are age-related; they are markers in life's maturation process. Other seasons are ushered in by a variety of life changes: a new marriage, career, the start of your family. Whatever the reason for the new season, it will touch all seven areas of life discussed earlier in this chapter.

On the most fundamental level, there are two kinds of seasons: *stable (or steady) seasons* and *seasons of change*. All of us can find examples of steady seasons in our lives in which certain aspects of life become predictable and are relatively easily managed.

For some, retirement is a steady season: routines are more easily adhered to and more firmly under the control of the retiree; job relocations no longer occur, changing positions and new bosses are in the past. Still, the steadiness of the season is not determined by the level of activity. Instead, it is determined by relative lack of flux and an awareness that life's conditions are at least temporarily reliable.

Seasons of change are quite different. They challenge the status quo and force us to test our perspectives and beliefs about how life works. New parents know all about seasons of change. Once the first child comes home, the household is permanently reordered: schedules change; sleep becomes scarce; spur-of-the-moment jaunts are harder to accomplish. Suddenly, husband and wife are focused on more than their own desires.

Seasonal changes always cost you something—comfort, familiarity, predictable routines, the assumption of security. Yet, they always give you something even more valuable, namely, an opportunity to grow. Before we move on, take a few moments to consider your current season. Use the questions in Figure 4 to explore and assess exactly where you are at this moment in your life.

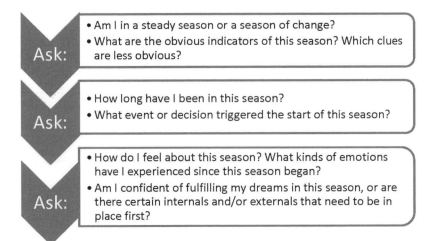

Figure 4

As already mentioned, some seasons are directly linked to age. Many characteristics of these seasons are experienced universally. For instance, those in their teens and twenties are typically preoccupied with exploring, experiencing, and discovering who they are apart from others.

This inner search has marked this age group generation after generation. That is not to say that the experiences of everyone in this age group are identical. Some twenty-somethings have a very clear vision of their life's purposes. For others, the picture is not so well defined. Regardless of individual progress, the formation of a clear sense of identity remains this age group's common quest.

The same is true of later decades. Whether you are in your twenties, thirties, or eighties, you are experiencing some markers of age transition common to nearly all people. At the root of it all is the search for meaning.

Finish the Season's Business

As we discussed in Chapter Three, we sometimes circumvent the search for meaning in order to avoid its messy emotional consequences. Here's the danger in postponing the search: the longer we sweep our questions under the rug of our *doing*, the more likely we are to struggle with our *being* later.

In the face of mounting disorientation, something will have to give, emotionally speaking. Confused and conflicting feelings can be stifled only so long before they bubble to the surface. The healthier approach is to deal with issues as they arise and keep a clean emotional slate as you transition from one season to another.

Whether the search for meaning erupts during unexpected events such as divorce, job loss, or catastrophic illness, the failure to wipe the emotional slate clean invariably produces a backlog of unresolved issues. I call this buildup "unfinished business." These are issues from your life story that were never adequately addressed and resolved.

> Unfinished business is a burr that attaches itself at the emotional level and becomes an irritant so persistent as to obscure your vision of life's big picture. If you're "saddled" with burrs, you can't be fully present to the moment called *now*. And, when *now* escapes you, your future suffers.[5]

In reality, everyone has some unfinished business stashed in the emotional basement. And everyone experiences emotion-generating periods of uncertainty, even late in life. The key to moving beyond these seasons is to address the issues early and thoroughly. Whether it's the first or the fifth time the challenge has surfaced, deal with it. Take ownership and find the value in the experience. Whether you feel pushed into a time of uncertainty or loss resulting from a job change, an unexpected relocation, the death of a loved one, or a financial setback, you can regain your equilibrium and your momentum.

If you own the situation, you empower yourself to recover and even make up for the time you thought had been lost forever.

THE POWER OF CHOICE

Would you like to have control over everything that could possibly affect you? Obviously, the question is rhetorical. There are many things we cannot control. You can teach your kids to do the right thing, but they *will* make mistakes. You can trust others to keep your secrets but, sooner or later, something you wanted held in confidence will be leaked. And, have you noticed that, no matter how carefully you invest, you cannot control the markets?

Sometimes, as the saying goes, "stuff happens." But, before you assume that you are a sitting duck in the crosshairs of happenstance, let me assure you that you are not. You can't control *everything* that happens, but you can control the choices you make in response to what happens.

The truth is that you are empowered to shape your personal history by the choices you make. No matter how good or bad the turn of events you are experiencing at this moment, your choices will determine your outcomes in the end.

Many of us read the previous sentence and experience a short circuit between our ears, because, for most of us, there is a noticeable disparity between the choices we have made and the outcomes we have achieved. We read our journals over and over; we stay up nights trying to figure how doing the "right" things led to the "wrong" results; we sigh and wonder when things will get better.

Think back to our scenario of the middle-school teacher. Our imaginary educator made excellent choices that ensured prepared-ness for a stellar teaching career. Dedicated and passionate, our teacher seemed destined for success.

However, other choices—unconscious choices—undermined what should have been a superb outcome. Driven by the fear of rejection, our imaginary teacher established a relational distance from students. Although this decision and the secondary decisions that sprang from it were made at the unconscious level, they were, nevertheless, functional *choices*. They led to specific actions (the withholding of relational intimacy) designed to achieve specific results (reduced vulnerability to rejection).

To the naked eye, our teacher "did everything right." Yet, unconscious choices hidden deep in the teacher's blind spot pro-duced the "wrong" outcomes. Instead of producing an emotion-al safety zone for the educator, they compromised destiny for everyone involved.

Such discrepancies between choices and outcomes are frus-trating precisely because they are caused by something we can-not see: the workings of the unconscious mind. The countless unconscious choices we make every day are hidden from view; yet they are effective in producing visible results. All too often, they are unexpected, unwanted results that broadcast our unspoken beliefs and values.

Do you remember when we talked about the ways in which we consciously or unconsciously describe ourselves? I asked if you describe yourself as being:

- Able or unable

- Likely or unlikely

- Wanted or unwanted

- Blessed or cursed

- Worthy or unworthy

These descriptions denote the choices we have made as to identity. Although these perspectives are often unconscious, we project them to others. For example: if I see myself as being unwanted, I will undoubtedly project that persona in my relationships, virtually entreating others to reject me. In other words, I will unknowingly choose to play a role that brings results I would never choose consciously to experience.

Think about the possibilities that could play out in a marriage, a family, a workplace. Do you see how untoward things could happen without your having a clue why? Take the scenario a step further: if you never realized your unconscious choice, how many times might the scenario repeat itself and how would that affect your life overall?

The answer is: *powerfully*. Because unconscious choices are hidden in our blind spots, they control us. Because we are unaware of our unconscious reactions, actions, and thoughts, we fail to recognize the role we play in the outcomes we experience. In ignorance, frustration, and self-protection we end up living inauthentic, self-justified lives. In order to make meaning of our circumstances, we use the compromised information we have; therefore, we blame others, we blame circumstances, we even blame deceased parents!

Remember, living from the inside out is to live a fully conscious, empowered life. It's an "inside job" that deals head-on with the issues and unfinished business that would otherwise perpetuate our unconscious choices and the outcomes they produce.

Inside-out living is the foundation of unfolding destiny.

YOUR NEXT CHOICE

"Oh no!" you exclaim. "I've been doomed by choices I didn't even know I made."

Not so. You haven't made your final choice yet! Your next choice is the one that really counts—and you can make it consciously.

It's a fact that your life story to this point is already written. But you can choose right now to own it. You can make your past a part of your personal history—a rich, textured, inspiring volume in which every page is meaningful!

ENDNOTES

1. Dr. Mark Chironna, *Live Your Dream* (Shippensburg, PA: Destiny Image, 2009), 48.

2. Mark J. Chironna, *You Can Let Go Now* (Nashville: Thomas Nelson, Inc., 2004), 120.

3. Ezra Greenspan, Lindeth Vasey, and John Worthen, eds., *The Cambridge Edition of the Works of D.H. Lawrence* (Cambridge, UK: Cambridge University Press, 2003), 13, http://books.google.com/books?id=IHSM6SIGi1AC &pg=PA13&lpg=PA13&dq=the+world+fears+a+ new+experience+more+than+it+fears+anything&sourc

e=bl&ots=cHxIkhwGdz&sig=GnB1OPNiv3Q1H0AVT
BAc0-uWUks&hl=en&ei=X_BYSsevMoL0sgOp
3pieCQ&sa=X&oi=book_result&ct=result&resnum=1
(accessed July 11, 2009).

4. Acts 2:1-41.

5. Dr. Mark Chironna, *Live Your Dream* (Shippensburg,
PA: Destiny Image, 2009), 66.

UNFOLD YOUR DESTINY

1. Of the seven areas of life discussed, which, in your opinion, are most developed in your life? Which do you feel are less so?

_____

_____

_____

_____

_____

_____

_____

2. What are some of the continuous and uninterrupted features of your life that give you a sense of connectedness to the past and the future?

_____

_____

_____

_____

_____

_____

_____

3. Have you become aware of any unconscious tendencies that have prompted choices in the past? How can
   you become more empowered in this area?

CHAPTER FIVE

Crystal-Clear Identity

"Seek first to understand,
and then to be understood."
—Stephen Covey,
Seven Habits of Highly Effective Teens

D O YOU REMEMBER THE classic Abbott and Costello routine, "Who's on First?" In the sketch, Costello asks Abbott for the names of the players on a certain team.

Abbott answers: "On the St. Louis team we have Who's on first; What's on second; I Don't Know's on third—"

Costello is perplexed. "That's what I want to find out. I want you to tell me the names of the fellas on the St. Louis team."

"I'm telling you—Who's on first; What's on second; I Don't Know's on third—"

"You know the fellas' names?"

"Yes," Abbott deadpans.

"Well then, who's playing first?"

"Yes."

"I mean the fella's name on first base," Costello begs.

"Who."

"The fella playin' first base for St. Louis."

Abbott nods affirmingly, "Who."

"The guy on first base!"

"Who is on first base."

"Well, what are you asking *me* for?" Costello pleads.

"I'm not asking you. I'm telling you. Who is on first."

"I'm asking *you* who's on first."

"That's the man's name," says Abbott.

"That's *whose* name?"

"Yes." Abbott replies.[1]

You get the idea. The absurdity of the communication makes for timeless comedy. However, real identity confusion is rarely funny. The questions *Who am I?* and *Who am I in relation to others?* are central to the human quest for meaning. Left unresolved, these questions become unyielding impediments to unfolding destiny.

Much identity confusion today is rooted in misconceptions about the value of being and the value of doing. Since World War II, performance has emerged as the primary emphasis of Western society. Simply stated, what you do and how well you do it trumps your inherent worth. Instead of living as human *beings*, we strive to become human *doings*.

Not surprisingly, we are most often judged by our achievements, skills, competencies, and education. These performance areas are important; however, applying them as ultimate standards of human value creates an imbalance. Yet we play into them and present ourselves artificially in order to game the system. We fully expect to be valued purely on the basis of what we do.

At the most fundamental level, these standards reflect our cultural predispositions since the mid-twentieth century. This framework for human value has diminished the perceived importance of our human essence, which is the very quality of *being*. Because of this imbalance, we have become performance-oriented; we seek to find our identities in what we do rather than discovering what we are called to do on the basis of who we are.

You can begin to see the ramifications of this perception gap. It affects us emotionally, psychologically, and socially. The drive to perform impacts our personal, professional, and family outcomes. Over the long term, it affects our quality of life: our physical well-being and mental health can be compromised. As a result, performance—the misplaced priority that drove the behavior in the first place—deteriorates.

Restoring the balance between your essence and what you do is one of the primary thrusts of this book. This emphasis is strong because reclaiming your essence as a human being reopens a destiny portal into the fully human, fully alive state you were created to inhabit.

> **essence** *noun*:
>
> The basic, real, and invariable nature of a thing or its significant individual feature or features… [In] *Philosophy*. the inward nature, true substance, or constitution of anything, as opposed to what is accidental, phenomenal, illusory, etc.[2]

YOUR WAY OF BEING

The imbalance between being and doing is an unsettled tension that juxtaposes your *way of being* with your capacity to perform. This exchange promotes self-deception and diverts the sound conduct of life. Your way of being is directly connected with your essence and is the progressive unfolding of your authentic God-given identity. It involves the process of both being and becoming.

Being is what ought to come naturally, but what is the importance of "becoming"? It's this: because we are human *beings* and not human *doings*, there is within each of us a desire to become the person we really are—the person we were created to be. (We'll see later that this is different from becoming someone we really aren't.) *Becoming* engages our power to recognize what is already within us, waiting to emerge. This emergence is realized when hindrances to the development and acceptance of authentic identity are removed.

This process is ongoing. Through it, we discover who we are apart from the perceptions of others. (This is similar to Jung's concept of individuation.)[3] This process involves our spiritual and psychological integration; it is the course of becoming whole by honoring the many parts of self and restoring them to alignment.

This wholeness in turn empowers us to bring unfettered uniqueness to the experience of living. When this process flows freely, others are able to draw strength from who we are. Encouraging the emergence of our own authentic identities encourages others to become the individuals they were born to be.

Consider this chapter your personal invitation to emerge in all the glory of your individuality and reclaim your way of being.

Be...Do...Have and Its Counterfeit

Being versus doing. The two are not mutually exclusive; when identity is clear, doing arises from being. The things you do are designed to flow from an understanding of the person you were created to be. This brings us back to your destiny code. It is the perfect representation of your potential and it includes the details of the purpose for which you were created. Your destiny code supports your function as a human being first and foremost.

That is not to say that you were designed to do nothing; you were created to do those things that support the unfolding of your destiny. Nor does it mean that everything you do attends strictly to your life; aspects of your unfolding destiny help to trigger the unfolding destinies of others. The point is that when your *doing* flows consistently from your *being*, you will discover that you can be, do, and have all that you imagine and more.

The order of these three verbs is specific:

- Be…

- Do…

- Have.

However, for the past three generations, the unconscious message has been: do…have…be. The misunderstanding begins here: If you perform well, you will have what you desire (*i.e.*, money, a mate, great "stuff," good health, terrific children). OK. That makes practical sense, but follow the corollary: If you have what you desire, you will become the person you want to be or believe you are supposed to be. Do you see the fallacy? (Does it remind you of Elise, who tried to become somebody else's idea of Elise?)

Although the misunderstanding seems subtle, the implications are profound. A gulf opens between the outcomes we desire and the ones we experience because we spend our lives trying to become someone else. We try to reshape ourselves into fictitious characters who we believe are better able to perform than we are and more deserving to reap future rewards. In other words, we wake up each day believing that "where we are" (and by implication, who we are) does not count.

This approach produces a chronic sense of under-performance that is based upon an always-moving, unreachable target. It erodes the trait of self-esteem (your favorable estimation of yourself) and prevents the development of the skill of self-esteem (the ability to accurately reconcile your emotions as they relate to your inherent value as a human being). Once your self-esteem is undermined, your self-worth is necessarily diminished. Worse still, the cycle is self-perpetuating because performance becomes the only standard of self-measurement. As a result, self-esteem and self-worth are continuously abased.

The *do…have…be* model also blinds us to our need for authentic affirmation, which includes not only affirmation for what we do, but also for the essence of who we are. This duality is obscured in a performance-oriented society. Consider the question we commonly ask children: *What do you want to be when you grow up?* The implication is stark: If you go to school, master your subjects, and perform well, you will eventually become "somebody." As for today, you are "nobody."

There is another consequence of performance orientation: just as we are trained to judge ourselves against inappropriate and deceptive standards, we learn to judge others the same way. We apply damning labels—words that create emotional barriers to unfolding destiny. This process is called *value-judging*. We'll talk more about it in the next chapter.

WAY OF BEING AND AUTHENTIC IDENTITY

The *do…have…be* model is the hamster-wheel approach to what you think you want. As long as you can keep the wheel spinning, you feel pretty good about yourself. But if you allow yourself an outside-the-wheel perspective, you will find that your exhausting efforts are leading you nowhere. In fact, your hard work will lead away from your dreams.

The hamster-wheel approach is fueled by misconceptions about identity. The frantic treading is a futile attempt to prop up self-esteem and inflate a lagging sense of self-worth. Those who understand their authentic identities and know who they are at their core don't saddle themselves with futile activity. Instead, they do what comes most naturally. They use their God-given gifts; therefore, good performance is effortless. It is a natural byproduct of their way of being. They are not trying to prove their worth;

instead, they are free to become all they were born to be—without stress, strife, restlessness, or fear of incompetence.

Your Authentic Identity

This is your true self, the "real you" free of all masks, cover-ups, and false projections. Your authentic identity reveals your God-given uniqueness and underpins your God-given destiny.[4]

With a clear sense of identity, you not only function effortlessly; you also become comfortable with your way of being. Instead of fighting to conceal perceived shortcomings, you drop the value judgments you might otherwise levy against yourself. You are free to see yourself objectively; you realize that, despite your flaws, you are capable, intelligent, competent, and equipped for a unique purpose. Because your view of self is affirming, you develop more fully; you increase your capacities and improve your performance, not through added toil, but through wholeness and the productivity it engenders.

When you turn your focus to your way of being rather than your doing, you begin to recognize your former addiction to your behaviors. Until you let go of your *need to perform*, you cannot know who you are at your core. Your attachment to performance-based identity will continue to obscure your essence.

Identity Checkpoint

1. Ask yourself this simple question: When was the last time I felt safe just being myself?

> 2. Describe the degree to which you feel safe being yourself (*i.e.*, never, rarely, occasionally, usually, always). How does your answer demonstrate acceptance or a lack of acceptance of the real you?

Affirmation Required

Affirmation is another popular word in the modern lexicon. When you affirm someone you make positive assertions about them; you confirm their worth; you uphold and support them; you foster healing and wholeness. At its root, the word *affirm* has to do with making firm or giving strength. This makes sense, because words create emotions or feelings; therefore, affirming words strengthen others and bolster the sense of self.

> **affirm** *verb*:
>
> 1. To state or assert positively; maintain as true
> 2. To confirm or ratify
> 3. To assert solemnly
> 4. To express agreement with or commitment to; uphold; support[5]

Words can also degrade or *infirm* others. To infirm is to diminish strength and foster fragmentation of self.

We can infirm individuals with our words. On a larger scale, society can be infirmed through words and the power of suggestion issuing from media, advertising, and the entertainment industry. This infirming process conveys a subliminal message of conditional love. We understand, even unconsciously, that if we perform well, we will be accepted and loved; but if we perform poorly, love and affirmation will be withheld.

By contrast, to be affirmed in your essence, rather than your performance, is an empowering aspect of unconditional love. When you are affirmed in who you are, you will not be easily infirmed when your performance slips. You become secure in the knowledge that your identity is not defined by your behaviors. Your behaviors are what you do, not who you are.

Affirmation also builds a healthy sense of self-esteem and safety. Because you are safe, you are free to be transparent. That transparency in turn allows relational intimacy, which generates added affirmation and the increased ability to give others the gift of affirmation you have already received.

Think for a moment about the relationships in your professional and personal life. Who are the people with whom you feel free to let down your guard? Is it the critical co-worker who takes every opportunity to diminish your talent? Probably not. Even if you are secure enough within yourself that your self-esteem does not rise and fall on the words of a detractor, you are likely to draw more careful boundaries when dealing with such an individual.

However, when you are in the company of an affirming friend, you become more transparent and open to interaction. The walls of self-protection come down, communication is open, and affirmation flows freely—to you and from you toward others.

Affirmation is truly a gift that must be both given and received. My prayer is that someone gave you that gift (the earlier and more often, the better). But what if those who should have affirmed you failed to do so? How are you to respond to the withholding of affirmation?

Please understand that if affirmation was withheld during your childhood, you felt the pain but were unable to make rational sense of it. Some of that unresolved pain remains with you as an adult, most likely at an unconscious level at which you can refuse to consciously feel it. However, until you are willing to feel the pain, you will not be able to heal.

Allow your pain to surface. As you do, remember that, most often, those who withhold affirmation from us do so for one reason: they themselves have received scarce affirmation. Acknowledge the wrong that was done to you; then choose to forgive. Not to do so is to hold both you and the offender in an emotional prison.

One final word about the gift of affirmation: it is a gift you receive from others, but it is also a gift you give yourself. Every time you embrace your being, your essence, your authentic identity, you affirm (add strength to) yourself.

Affirmation Checkpoint

A simple question can reveal a great deal about the degree to which you were affirmed early in life. Ask yourself: *When was the first time (or any time) I was affirmed, not for something I did, but for my essence?*

Describe your experience.

SEVEN SECRETS TO UNFOLDING DESTINY

SOCIETY'S AFFIRMATION DEFICIT

The truth is that almost none of us have been adequately affirmed for who we are. This societal "infirmity" is rooted in the culture of performance, which is in large part, a product of secular humanism, "...an outgrowth of eighteenth century enlightenment rationalism and nineteenth century freethought...."[6]

The tenets of humanism have been stated in a series of Humanist Manifestos, the first of which was issued in 1933. By the end of World War II, secular humanism had become the prevailing Western philosophy.

---

humanism *noun*:

A doctrine, attitude, or way of life centered on human interests or values; *especially* a philosophy that usually rejects supernaturalism and stresses an individual's dignity and worth and capacity for self-realization through reason.[7]

---

secular humanism *noun*:

Humanism; *especially* humanistic philosophy viewed as a nontheistic religion antagonistic to traditional religion.[8]

Secular humanism ostensibly seeks to develop and promote the individual and his or her human potential. It does this in part by establishing relativism, the belief that absolutes do not exist and decisions can therefore be made on a situational basis. In other words, the right choice is whatever is expedient in a given situation (the definition of *right* being entirely subjective and malleable, as circumstances dictate).

By elevating human effort, situational ethics, and the dictates of science to the level of ultimate authority, secular humanism creates an environment in which the affirmation of essence is withheld, authentic identity is undermined, and the drive to perform and even perfect oneself is perpetuated.

It is easy to see why modern society cannot offer unconditional love. Instead, it praises what we do before it affirms who we are. Although educators work hard, help students succeed, and often serve powerfully as mentors, the overriding secular humanist philosophy reinforces society's affirmation deficit. We train students to prove themselves on the basis of their actions rather than addressing their ways of being. We inadvertently overlook the individual's connectedness with the inner aspects of unfolding destiny.

In this context, we can also understand why we feel uncomfortable when others affirm our essence. We are simply not accustomed to being affirmed in this way; it exposes our unconscious beliefs and deep-rooted fears that unconditional love is unavailable. Affirmation of essence also tends to seem "mushy." Emotionally speaking, it disarms us and seems to be anything but strengthening. Even more threatening, perhaps, is the fact that genuine affirmation cuts beneath our protective masks and lowers our emotional guardrails.

IDENTITY BASICS

You have already asked yourself the question, *When was the last time I felt safe just being myself?* If you have *never* felt safe being yourself, it may be that you don't know who you really are. But, don't despair; this common malady is curable!

We are addressing the issue for very important reasons. For one, until your authentic identity is recognized, your destiny will be log-jammed somewhere between your heart and your head. In other words, your conscious dreams and desires will be sabotaged by your unconscious tendencies.

Second, you will be prone to projecting false images of yourself in order to protect against the possibility of rejection. (This is what I mean when I refer to the wearing of masks.) False images prevent steady forward movement because they undermine purpose and prevent relational intimacy. In a sense, these masks are pathways to an unsustainable parallel life; in the end, they fail to protect and only drive you far afield of your destiny.

Third, identity confusion causes us to seek safety in counter-productive ways. Instead of embracing those who would empower us with truth (about ourselves, our thoughts, our endeavors), we embrace those who pacify us. We take temporary shelter in denial; it enables us to postpone needed change by living what are essentially illusions. Instead of finding safety, we experience further damage to our well-being, self-interests, and life outcomes.

Before we delve further into false self-images, let's refresh our memories of three key terms discussed in the Introduction.

IDENTITY ELEMENTS	DEFINITION	STATEMENT
Self-concept	Your global evaluation of who you perceive your-self to be. A big-picture checklist that covers such details as your role in society, your status, and other over-arching characteristics of your person. Some of these features are measured against so-called norms.	*I am a married Hispanic woman, the mother of three, and a schoolteacher. I am an athletic person who runs the marathon each year. I am successful in my profession and expect career advancement in the coming years.*

IDENTITY ELEMENTS	DEFINITION	STATEMENT
Self-esteem	A snapshot of self that is evaluated and experienced at an affective level (involves feelings). Self-esteem is both a trait and a skill. It can be described as the degree to which your view of yourself is favorable.	*Although I am blessed with marriage, children, and a gratifying career, I feel less qualified for these roles than some of my friends and loved ones. They seem to have it all together in ways I don't think I can accomplish.*
Self-worth	Self-worth is a value statement formulated through your cognitive skills. It expresses the extent to which you believe you are deserving of being respected by others and by yourself. It is your perceived value as a person based upon what you believe or believe you know about yourself.	*I am a wife, mother, and professional educator, yet I feel unworthy of these gifts (and the love and respect they engender), as though they were granted to me by some mistake or oversight. I am working hard and hope to be worthy of these gifts someday.*

Figure 5

IDENTITY, SELF-ESTEEM, AND SELF-IMAGE

Masks, projections, self-image—these are names for the diversions we consciously and unconsciously use to conceal the parts of our authentic identities we find threatening.

Have you seen the classic British sitcom *Keeping Up Appearances?* The main character, Hyacinth Bucket, works hard to impress the upper crust of society and wind her way into their circles. She insists that her last name is pronounced *Bouquet;* she also holds fancy candlelight dinners, runs her respectable husband ragged, and distances herself from her rough-and-tumble relatives.

Hyacinth's best efforts fail miserably. She is always found out and humiliated in the most public of ways. No one buys the images she tries to project; in fact, they think less of her than they might have otherwise. Because of her antics, she makes no real progress, but experiences endless frustration. Instead of attracting the "right people," she drives away everyone she meets!

Hyacinth's behavior—the chronic projection of a crafted self-image—reflects our societal misunderstanding of self-esteem. Remember, healthy self-esteem is the favorable, from-the-inside-out feeling about oneself. It is a trait and a skill held in varying degrees by each of us. Self-image, on the other hand, is an imitation; it is a concocted version of self that we want others to accept as being real. It is not based in authentic, God-given identity; it is the product of self-effort and it produces, at best, a form of borrowed, second-hand living.

You can think of self-image as a hologram, a seeming reality created with nothing more than the play of light. We direct the light to reveal the parts we create or choose to display while keeping the parts we don't like under the cover of darkness. Because our legitimate needs are unmet, we are unconsciously driven by them. We compensate for this inner emptiness with toys designed to impress others and allay our pain.

Instead of valuing our uniqueness, we exchange it for a counterfeit image cobbled together with features we think will be well received. The process is self-perpetuating; the longer we continue to project false images, the more unconscious and controlling they become. They are also self-limiting; they box us into scripts of our own making and divert us from paths of unique destiny.

We cannot become the people we were meant to be until we let go of the people we think we *should* be. Like Hyacinth, our masks will always be found out. The toys will fail to cover our neediness; our braggadocio or false humility will wear thin; our unconscious communication—the expressions, words, body language, and choices that express what is deep in our hearts—will eventually betray the finest of disguises and leave us more fragmented than we were before.

THE REAL THING

Marvin Gaye and Tammi Terrell sang the 1968 classic: "Ain't Nothing Like the Real Thing...."[9] The lyrics explain that photos and letters from loved ones cannot substitute for their presence. The song describes the writer's desire for the "real thing": "I play the game, a fantasy, I pretend but I'm not in reality, I need the shelter of your arms to comfort me."[10]

The genuine always trumps the counterfeit. When you understand who you are at your core, you can embrace the genuine. Your identity cannot be separated from your destiny. When you know who you are, you uncork the understanding of what you are called to do. This in turn releases access to what you need to accomplish your life's purpose.

Instead of performing to prove your worth, you can be who you were created to be. Out of that being, your doing flows organically. This is fully conscious living. When your life unfolds this way, you are fully alive. You are present to the moment (opportunities are maximized); you are open to constructive input and change (your capacities can be increased); you are comfortable in your own skin (and others are at ease with you).

115

The energy that might have been dedicated to the propping up of masks is now freed up for productive endeavors. The more productive you become (not as an act of performance, but of destiny fulfillment), the higher your level of self-esteem and the more you are able to affirm others.

There is nothing like the real thing. When you own your identity, you do what comes naturally and you do it seamlessly. Tomorrow is no longer approached with dread; each day becomes an adventure and another opportunity to live your dream.

> Don't ask yourself what the world needs—ask yourself what makes you come alive, and then do it. Because what the world needs is people who have come alive.[11]
>
> —*Harold Thurman Whitman*

REALITY CHECKS AND WAKE-UP CALLS

So is living your dream like living in a dream world? Not exactly. The commitment to being real comes with challenges of its own. The reality is that most of us will go through a crisis or two (or more).

But life's crises aren't all doom and gloom. They have a way of advancing growth and developing authentic identity. For one thing, crises (including crises of meaning, which we'll examine in Chapter Six) tend to slow us down to the speed of real life. We become more attuned to being than doing. During crises, we reevaluate our priorities and often become aware of our disguises.

The resulting growth is beneficial. We become more authentic, flexible, touchable, gentler, and compassionate. We rediscover dormant values—the ones that were waiting to emerge from below the surface of our conscious lives. As these pieces of our destiny codes are unearthed, they become tools we can use to unfold destiny.

When we are open to the "real things" in life, including the unexpected obstacles, challenges, uncertainties, setbacks, and losses, we become better balanced and better equipped to fulfill our destinies. Even the successes and accomplishments—the high points that fail to fulfill but instead leave us feeling empty—end up serving a valuable purpose. These wake-up calls alert us to the unconscious diversions that have crept into our lives. They sound the alarm and restore us to our destiny paths.

Few people find wake-up calls inviting or remotely attractive. Crises have the appearance of interruptions; they come in the midst of chaos or strike in a seemingly steady season. As off-putting as they are, they are components of destiny development. Because they help position you to honor your destiny code, they can be the beginning of your journey toward the practice of your true destiny.

UNFOLDING DESTINY MEASUREMENTS

Internal balance congruence is the harmony of your internal and external pursuits. When your words, thoughts, and actions are moving along the same track and your speech and body language correspond with your intent, you experience greater ease in accomplishing your goals. When your feelings and goals are harmonized, your intent produces your desired results. It is the kind of fully conscious living we have talked about. This coherence of inner life and outer experience promotes the flow of destiny.

But is this coherence measurable? The answer is, yes. Although life's signals are layered, there is a way to calculate the level of coherence and assess how effectively your destiny is unfolding. It comes down to the degree to which your life combines certain essential elements, including:

- *Your inner search for meaning*—Are you an active meaning-maker or a bystander in your own life?

- *Your mission quest (essentially, your calling)*—Are you actively pursuing your calling or are you waiting for your future to arrive?

- *Your conscious sense of connectedness to your destiny*—Do you see your destiny as being uniquely yours? Do you believe you are empowered to achieve it or powerless to affect your outcomes?

- *The patterns and cycles of change you experience over time*—Do you recognize and appreciate seasonal shifts? Are you averse to change or do you actively seek the fields of opportunity that are revealed in times of change?

- *The external validation and confirmation of your highest pursuits*—Do you believe your endeavors are directed from within? If so, are you experiencing positive external consequences and circumstances related to those pursuits?

- *The rewards your pursuit yields*—To what extent does your *being* direct your *doing*? Are your efforts reaping appropriate rewards?

When you embrace your authentic identity, you foster the coordinated function of all of these moving parts. Consider your answers to the questions asked and determine whether and to what degree they indicate the fully alive, active pursuit of unfolding destiny.

Then, whatever your conclusion, take your power and use it. Tomorrow is another opportunity for unfolding destiny.

ENDNOTES

1. Abbott and Costello, *The Naughty Nineties* (1945), http://www.youtube.com/watch?v=sShMA85pv8M (accessed July 14, 2009).

2. "Essence," Dictionary.com, Dictionary.com Unabridged, v. 1.1 (Random House, Inc.), http://dictionary.reference.c om/browse/essence (accessed July 14, 2009).

3. C.J. Jung, *Dreams* (London: Routledge Classics, 2002), 108, http://books.google.com/books?id=SWvdQyo _ZX0C&printsec=frontcover&dq=carl+jung#v=one page&q=individuation&f=false.

4. Dr. Mark Chironna, *Live Your Dream* (Shippensburg, PA: Destiny Image, 2009), x.

5. "Affirm," Dictionary.com, Dictionary.com Unabridged, v. 1.1 (Random House, Inc.), http://dictionary.reference. com/browse/affirm (accessed July 14, 2009).

6. Fred Edwords, "What Is Humanism?" *American Humanist Association* (1989 and 2008), http://www. americanhu- manist.org/who_we_are/about_humanism/What_is_H umanism (accessed July 14, 2009).

7. "Humanism," Merriam-Webster Online Dictionary (2009), Merriam-Webster Online, http://www.merriam-webster.com/dictionary/humanism (accessed July 14, 2009).

8. "Secular humanism," Merriam-Webster Online Dictionary (2009), Merriam-Webster Online, http://www.merriam-webster.com/dictionary/secular humanism (accessed July 14, 2009).

9. Nickolas Ashford and Valerie Simpson, "Ain't Nothing Like the Real Thing," performed by Marvin Gaye and Tammi Terrell (Tamla Records, 1968), 7-inch single.

10. Nickolas Ashford and Valerie Simpson, "Ain't Nothing Like the Real Thing," lyrics viewed on SoundTrack Lyrics Source, stlyrics.com, © 2002-2009, http:// www.stlyrics.com/lyrics/thebigchill/aintnothingliketherealthing.htm (accessed July 16, 2009).

11. Harold Thurman Whitman, "Quotable Quote" (Goodreads, Inc.), http://www.goodreads.com/quotes/show/25920 (accessed August 25, 2009).

UNFOLD YOUR DESTINY

1. To what degree does your life currently demonstrate the "be, do, have" model? What factors contribute to your assessment?

2. To what degree do you sense an affirmation deficit and how can you resolve it in a forward-moving way? How can you ensure against perpetuating this deficit in the lives of loved ones?

3. Over the next days and weeks, take a written "inventory" regarding your self-concept, self-esteem, self-worth, and any use of self-protecting masks. Try to trace back the development of these elements over the course of your life. Then finish any unfinished business you find.

PART
II

REPACK YOUR BAGS

(How to Unplug Unconscious Tendencies)

CHAPTER SIX

Two Sides of the Judgment Coin

"Judging is a lonely job in which a man is,
as near as may be, an island entire."
—Abe Fortas

A BE FORTAS' TERM ON the United States Supreme Court ended unceremoniously, yet his words aptly describe the lonely position of every judge who presides over cases brought before the courts. What an enormous responsibility it is to judge matters of law!

The isolation Fortas describes can also be experienced by people like us: self-appointed judges who wear no robes, but stand on the invisible precedents that are lodged in the unconscious mind. These hidden standards govern our thoughts, choices, and actions and cause us to hand down independent judgments over situations and people, including ourselves.

Such value judgments stand independent of the truth and pack a punch. They are not a twenty-first-century phenomenon, but originated millennia ago in a garden named *Eden* where history's earliest law was decreed: *"You can eat from any tree in the garden, except from the Tree-of-Knowledge-of-Good-and-Evil. Don't eat from it. The moment you eat from that tree, you're dead."*[1]

The divine message could not have been clearer. Yet, a cleverly crafted conversation soon parsed the warning and set the stage for history's greatest downfall. The dialogue went something like this:

"So," the deceiver probed, "did I hear that *all* the trees in this garden are off limits to you folks?"

The woman responded swiftly, adding a flourish of her own, "No, just that tree in the center of the garden. God said we couldn't eat from it *or even touch it* without dying."

Aware that the truth had already been tweaked, the opportunistic serpent took license with it and offered a rationale of his own: "Those apples won't kill you. God doesn't want you to eat them because He doesn't want to share all He knows with you. He doesn't want any competition."

The woman entertained the serpent's suggestions and began to judge the situation by them. She thought, *Wow, this guy's right! Why shouldn't I know everything? Besides, the apples look delicious. Why wouldn't I eat one?*

Her mind was made up. Eve took a bite and shared the apple with her husband, Adam. Instantly, the two felt ashamed of their nakedness. They hid from God, who knew everything that happened.

Because He loved them, He challenged their shame. "Who said you were naked?" He asked. "Have you been eating from that tree I warned you about?"

At that moment, the finger-pointing began.

The man exclaimed to God, "You know that woman You gave me? She started this mess!"

Squirming on the hot seat of judgment, the woman returned a verdict of her own: "No way! It's that serpent! He's to blame!"[2]

From that day to this, we humans have judged situations and people on the basis of flawed information. We have also pointed the finger of accusation in the hopes of shifting the unbearable weight of shame onto someone else's shoulders. We have judged one another and ourselves relentlessly—and for reasons we have rarely understood.

The Venom of Value-Judging

Value-judging is the making of independent judgments. These are the faulty verdicts we hand down to others purely on the basis of our subjective definitions of *good* and *bad* in given situations. These opinions are untrustworthy because they are grounded in unconscious deceptions, misperceptions, and misunderstandings of the truth.

Independent judgments are, by definition, divisive. First and foremost, they divide us internally. We inaccurately judge ourselves, making off-hand yet impactful remarks such as: "I'm stupid"; "I'm unattractive"; "I'm unlovable." These assertions reveal our confusion about destiny and self-worth. They show that, somewhere between the head and the heart, a split has occurred—a rift that separates us from the experience of unconditional acceptance. Self-esteem fluctuates unpredictably, soaring one day and plunging the next. Fluid circumstances that have little to do with our value as human beings begin to dictate how we feel about self.

Independent judgments also breed division in relationships. Blame games and other defensive behaviors drive wedges between us. Couples engage in fault-finding, rending the very fabric of their love and building emotion-reinforced walls of division that undermine other areas of life. Children shift blame by lying to their parents and end up feeling isolated from the ones who love them most.

When we make value judgments, we impede healing and growth. Our unresolved issues pile up higher and our struggles with shame intensify. Day by day, we add new layers of false identity to conceal our "dis-eases." And as long as we embrace value-judging, we subject ourselves and others to its eroding power.

This power issues from the root cause of value-judging, which is guilt. It is the sense that blame is due, not merely for wrong actions, but for the failure to measure up to man-made (and virtually unattainable) standards, the subjective concept of *good* mentioned earlier.

Regardless of who is on the receiving end of value-judging, guilt continues to divide from within, creating chronic incongruence between the head and heart. Desires and actions become mismatched. Feelings betray cover-ups and expose the flaws we would rather conceal. Errant thoughts oppose our best intentions. Revealing words disclose the thoughts buried deep inside. Ultimately, faulty choices and actions impede our progress.

If guilt is the root of value-judging, fear is the fruit. We develop the sense that our shortfalls will lead to loss and further shame. This fear isolates us from the people, situations, and opportunities that would otherwise flow as a natural expression of our life's purposes. We become increasingly uncomfortable in our own skin and develop self-hatred. As we attempt to escape our authentic identities, the unconditional acceptance we crave becomes increasingly inaccessible. The more we morph outward presentations of self (which we do to ensure "safe" outcomes), the more we unconsciously forbid ourselves the undergirding power of affirmation.

This progression results in increasing opaqueness and isolation. Instead of facing up to our imperfections, we find ways to conceal the "evidence" that seems stacked against us. We self-protect by resisting beneficial input (including sound correction and thoughtful advice); instead, we build and hold ourselves captive in fortresses of self-justification.

Refusing to accept life's imperfections and our own flaws, we become habitually critical of ourselves and others. We lack transparency, therefore others can't see the "real" people we are. We become one-dimensional and inadvertently conceal even our best qualities. In time, others receive from us nothing more than judgment. We unconsciously transmit the verdict that says, "You are at least as flawed as I am and maybe worse."

Value-judging is isolating on every level. Others sense even our unspoken judgments and protect themselves against not-so-subtle barbs. Although we ultimately want to be liked, these dynamics cause others to withdraw from us.

In the end, the sentences we pass on them fall upon us.

Value-Judging Checkpoint

Take a moment to consider whether blame games and other defensive behaviors are driving a wedge in your relationships. To help your assessment, explore any ways in which you have judged yourself or others severely.

Conscious and Unconscious Judgments

Not all forms of judgment are negative. In most nations, a legal system requires the passing of judgment. These assessments are crucial to a lawful society; without them, anarchy would prevail.

As individuals, we are also called to make sound judgments. We use our faculties to judge wisely and ensure healthy living. We discipline our children so they can live productive lives; we discern whether their friends are helpful or harmful to their well-being. We hold one another accountable to truth and propriety in business and personal relationships. We rightly object to the destructive actions of others, protecting ourselves and those who are vulnerable from unnecessary harm.

These are conscious, daily decisions made by applying fact and larger truths to the situations at hand. We make these decisions consciously and with good intent. We are not called to point the finger at everyone who fails to meet our expectations; but neither are we called to ignore injustice, criminal activity, or predatory behaviors. It is appropriate to judge actions and assess outcomes in order to make sound decisions.

Value-judging, on the other hand, occurs at the unconscious level. It reveals what is in the heart, not of the one being judged, but of the person issuing the verdict. It discloses our ability or refusal to accept and cope with reality as it is. It reveals the degree to which we feel threatened by what we cannot control and it exposes our unspoken fears of being on the receiving end of judgment.

A simple story provides a stunning example of value-judging. A businessman intently reading his morning paper was riding the New York City subway to work when an unkempt man with three small children entered the subway car.

As the train continued on its way, the children scampered about the car talking loudly, calling out to their father, and disrupting the relative quiet of the businessman's "reading room."

Annoyed at the imposition and the father's seeming ineptitude, the businessman glared at him. The father, however, seemed oblivious to the rider's mounting anger and equally unaware of his children's wild behavior.

Finally, the businessman asked the father, "Sir, don't you see that your children are out of control and disturbing other commuters? Why don't you do something about their awful conduct?"

The father looked vacantly at the man and replied, "Forgive me. We are just returning home from the hospital. We've been there since the day before yesterday. My wife passed away early this morning and I'm trying to figure out how to tell my children that their mother is gone."

You can imagine the businessman's gasp at the man's heartbreaking story and the realization that he'd completely misread the situation. The businessman's assessment was entirely based on his own preconceived notions and unconscious beliefs about how people on the subway "ought" to behave.

When we judge inappropriately, we reveal the belief that acceptance is unavailable to us. Therefore, we withhold acceptance from others. Instead of coming to terms with real situations, people, events, and behaviors, we attempt to gain control by criticizing them. These judgments occur at the unconscious level where our definitions of *good* and *bad* are housed. Without realizing what we are doing, we become a law unto ourselves.

The illegitimate authority we attempt to wield is defensive. It is designed to protect us from those we believe to be untrustworthy. For many who have suffered rejection, abandonment, and abuse, the rule of thumb has become "Trust no one." But, even if we have not been abused, we make decisions every day about who deserves access to our hearts.

I do not advocate opening your heart to everyone who crosses your path. Experience and sound judgment will reveal the degree of openness that is appropriate in a given situation. However, affirming relationships are built on a level of openness that will promote a healthy exchange and an appropriate degree of intimacy.

On an unconscious level, the amount of access we allow is directly tied to the level of our acceptance of the situations, events, and other people we encounter. When acceptance is at work, the resulting openness permits information, affirmation, emotion, trust, and commitment to be exchanged. This give and take creates an environment in which all parties can advance toward their respective destinies.

Depending on upbringing and other life experiences, this exchange can cause discomfort. Long-forgotten, unrecognized, and unhealed emotional wounds can cause us to fear emotional exposure. Unchecked, this fear can then prompt us to close off access to our hearts and shield our hurts, much the way we would protect physical sore spots.

Instead of risking reinflammation of our emotional wounds, we erect gauntlets to test the love and trustworthiness of others. Too often, we withdraw our hearts from view and prevent the very exposure that brings the healing, affirmation, and freedom we long to experience.

CHOICES, FEELINGS, AND THE UNCONSCIOUS

If value-judging occurs unconsciously, how can you know when you are doing it? Depending on the degree to which your conscience operates freely (unhindered by masks, self-protection, and misperceptions) you are able to recognize the value judgments when you issue them. You can probably remember times when you've said something hurtful and felt the tug of regret in your heart.

Yet, even when value judgments are hidden in our blind spots, we can uncover them by monitoring our emotions. Feelings such as anger, self-pity, and jealousy often expose our value-judging and are powerful indicators of the unconscious at work.

Think about the last time someone "made you mad." Did your feelings rush to the surface in a blinding torrent? In that emotional moment, could you identify the source of your reaction? Did anger happen *to you* or did you have power *over it?*

Chances are, these questions never arose in the heat of whatever conflict triggered your most recent bout of anger. Because of the way anger and other emotions erupt, we tend to believe that they are beyond our control. Yet, anger is a choice.

This seeming hair-trigger response doesn't happen *to you;* it is chosen *by you.* When someone flips the switch on your defense mechanisms, you are faced with a series of questions:

- Will I be carried off by my emotions?

- Should I justify myself?

- Can I forgo the emotional clamor in my soul, or will I pass judgment in the hope of proving myself right?

> The strongest principle of growth lies in human choice.[3]
>
> —George Eliot

Even when hurtful things are said or done to us, anger remains just one of many available choices. We can explode in tirades and decry the inconsideration of our offenders. Or, we can take a breath, regroup, and say, "I never realized that you felt that way. How can we make this right?" If we will stop the emotional clock long enough to learn something about ourselves and others, we can choose to deescalate damaging interactions and advance the relationships that are so important to destiny fulfillment.

Again, this has to do with the ability to receive and offer unconditional acceptance. If I can accept myself, I will be more likely to accept you. If I accept you, I have opened the door to cooperation and healing. But, this process doesn't happen in a vacuum; it takes effort and intentionality in the context of relationship. In the heat of conflict, we need to recognize what we are feeling. Then, having developed this conscious awareness of our emotions, we can assess them, adjust them, and *choose* acceptance.

This moving from the unconscious into the conscious realm creates an environment in which our progress moves from the theoretical to the practical. If you say something that trips my wire, I must deal with the feelings that ensue. I must also deal with the reasons for those feelings.

Remember: as long as we operate in the unconscious, we are controlled by it. When we look the issue in the face, however, we retain control of our choices and are empowered to give and receive acceptance.

When we move situations out of the unconscious realm, our chances of making sound choices increase exponentially. That does not mean we will never choose anger. However, we know the consequences ahead of time. On the one hand, we know that if we choose anger, we will withdraw, withhold acceptance, and cause further alienation in the relationship. On the other hand, if we reject anger and choose to remain open, we can accept the reality of altercations and work through them to produce better outcomes and promote the unfolding of destiny.

Whether they are made consciously or unconsciously, our choices *will* determine our outcomes.

VALUE-JUDGING CHECKLIST

The human conscience was designed to make us aware of inappropriate thoughts and behaviors. We have seen that a conscious examination of our feelings can provide additional insight into the value judgments we make. There is still another value-judgment detector: it is our behavior. Let's examine nine specific behaviors that help us to recognize when we are engaged in value-judging.

Criticism

We are often more critical of ourselves than of anyone else; yet our critical viewpoints will always spill over into our relationships with others. This kind of criticism is not typically a reasoned evaluation of an area in need of improvement, but an indicator of value-judging.

For example, if you harbor feelings of inadequacy that are exacerbated by the proficiency of your staff member, you'll want to monitor your interaction in the relationship. Let's suppose that this staffer makes an honest mistake and causes a project to be delayed. Correcting the staffer and explaining the consequences of the misstep would constitute responsible actions. Sound judgment is beneficial in the long term, ensuring better outcomes for the firm and providing the kind of leadership that promotes individual success.

However, if you accuse this honest staffer of envying your success and trying to make you look bad, you are probably making a value judgment. The criticism is based, not on truth, but on some impetus from the unconscious mind. This input is generated by deception or a fundamental misunderstanding of the truth. In this example, an unconscious fear of failure or of being superseded is driving the exchange. You end up reaping the brunt of confrontation, because the value judgment reveals more about you than it reveals about anyone else.

Comparison

When we are unclear about our unique identities or fail to value our inherent self-worth, we diminish ourselves and become driven by the need for approval. As a result, we measure ourselves against those we believe are receiving the approval we crave. We think and say things like: "Pete is smarter than I am," "If only I had Marilyn's pretty face," or "I wish I had Tom's family life." Sometimes, our comparisons seem to be more positive: "My house is so clean compared to Sue's. How can her husband stand it?" Regardless of how we construct our comparisons, they are value judgments that overlook two important facts:

1. Our self-worth is inherent and not measured against anyone else.

2. Each of us has a unique combination of strengths and weaknesses.

There is no earthly ideal against which we can accurately assess ourselves; and even if there were, comparison would be a self-sabotaging venture.

Competition

If we compare ourselves with others, we will eventually compete with them. When we compete in unhealthy ways, we fabricate scenarios in which we hope to create new sources of approval. What we are really trying to do is to soothe the ache of the seemingly unfavorable comparisons we have drawn.

This competition is not always overt; often it prompts behaviors that seem unconnected to other people. The buying of expensive "toys" can fall into this covert category of competition. Almost without realizing it, we can feel compelled to make unnecessary or extravagant purchases. These could be unconscious attempts to level the playing field in regard to the unfavorable comparisons we harbor.

For example, if you believe Jeanine's life is more exciting or fulfilling than yours, you might find ways to surpass her. The actions you take might seem unrelated to Jeanine, yet serve to elevate or inflate your self-image so that it compares more favorably to your mental picture of her. You might buy a certain car or even consider plastic surgery. These unhealthy competitive acts reveal your value judgments about Jeanine and, more importantly, about yourself. (Although the competition we're discussing here is not of the sports variety, it is possible to use sports as a tool of unhealthy competition.)

Sarcasm

Sarcasm is a foil for anger. When we are sarcastic, we reveal disdain for another person, organization, or situation. This disdain is a value judgment. Through sarcasm, we can express our anger and other negative emotions without being transparent and open to the target of our remarks. Instead of stating an observation directly, we lace it with attitude and even humor. This delivery disarms others; it is unexpected, sends multiple messages, and often camouflages our intent. It also seeks to inflict a measure of pain, thereby revealing the belief that the victim of our sarcasm is deserving of being hurt.

Mind Reading

The mind reading I'm talking about has nothing to do with what psychics claim to do. Instead of reading someone's actual thoughts, it has more to do with reading *into* someone's thoughts on the basis of your own perceptions, insecurities, or emotional blind spots. This is a form of value-judging that is based on faulty assumptions of what you *think* is on someone else's mind. Often, it attributes to others the thoughts that you entertain (see *projection*, below). Like all value judgments, it is independent; in other words, it is not based in truth.

Assuming

To assume is to create and accept as truth a scenario that is based on limited, biased, or faulty information. Therefore, our assumptions about people and situations are unreliable. We judge people's thoughts and values, and the ways in which we expect them to react to a variety of circumstances. We often make assumptions about their behaviors (especially toward us) and about their gifted-ness (or lack thereof). Because of our misguided assumptions, we are often surprised by their successes and failures, choices and actions, and even their feelings about us.

Relational Stress

Do you know someone who has an uncanny tendency to generate tension? Some people seem prone to chronic relational difficulty, regardless of the setting and the people with whom they interact. Such recurring patterns of friction in personal and professional interaction are indicators of ongoing value-judging. Relational stress can be based on misgivings about self-worth and the value others place on being in relationship with us. Relational stress can result from the fear of relational failure (the assumption that our relationships are doomed). Rather than be "victimized" through desertion or abandonment, we unconsciously choose to end relationships on our terms; we sabotage them and avoid outcomes that are outside of our control.

Projection

This is a powerful self-defense mechanism by which we project our undesirable thoughts, motives, desires, feelings, and other aspects of self onto others, ascribing to them what is hidden inside of us. It is an unconscious effort to deny the features of self we perceive to be threatening. Projection enables us to avoid the difficult emotions these features would present if we were to acknowledge them. Projection is often in play when we prejudge people or situations, make assumptions, or engage in mind reading.

Labeling

This indicator of value-judging categorizes others according to arbitrary standards. We label individuals and groups (religions, political parties, races, and cultures) that fail to "measure up" in our estimation. We are more prone to labeling others when we our-selves feel unaffirmed. By diminishing them, we artificially and temporarily inflate self-image. This momentary relief has a high cost: labels are words and, because words create feelings, they can cause injury. When we label others, we are publishing value judg-ment against them.

VALUE-JUDGING AND "UNFINISHED BUSINESS"

As you read earlier, unfinished business involves issues from your life story that were never adequately addressed and resolved. These issues attach themselves at an emotional level, playing back the old scripts and events of your life in new and seemingly unrelat-ed circumstances.

For the sake of discussion, let's create a scenario: Imagine that you were jilted at the altar. The pain of the rejection you suffered was so great that you failed to deal with it adequately. Instead, you covered over the wound and moved on. Now, with the traumatic experience in your rear-view mirror, you meet a great guy and he pops the question. Outwardly, you are happily engaged; but on an unconscious level, you are fearful of repeating your earlier experience.

Your new fiancé concludes a business trip. The two of you planned ahead of time to get together on the night of his return. You rent a film you know he wants to see and you order his favorite takeout. When your fiancé deplanes, he calls to say that he's completely exhausted from the trip and has an early debriefing the next day. He explains that he'd just as soon get some rest and see you tomorrow.

Absent any evidence that he is untrustworthy, your unfinished business could cause you to form a value judgment: *He is not really exhausted. He is avoiding me. He no longer loves me and is planning to jilt me.* Instead of accepting an innocent cancellation at face value and encouraging your fiancé to get some needed rest, you could allow your disappointment to bloom as outright anger. Even if you wisely avoid an emotional outburst, simmering resentment could poison your thought processes and your relationship.

Although your fiancé knows about your previous engagement and all the pain it caused, he probably doesn't realize that he is walking into an emotional mine field of what I call *hidden spots.* These are feelings-driven places where you harbor old fears, resentments, pains, and anger. Those who tread there risk the wrath of an unconscious reflex spurred by an unhealed wound. These "circumstances do not create [your] pain. Circumstances merely trigger the pain that is already there, hiding just below the surface of [your] awareness."[4]

Remember that what happens at the unconscious level controls us, in part because we are blind to it. The potential for unfinished business to sabotage our lives cannot be underestimated. In our movie-night scenario, an inappropriate response could set the stage for what you fear most—a fiancé with cold feet! Your unfounded distrust of him could, over time, produce in him a well-founded distrust of you.

The unfinished business that continues to operate on an unconscious level causes us to repeat the very experiences we seek to avoid.

Unfinished Business Checkpoint

Take a moment to identify hidden spots in which you carry anger and resentment. Be specific and consider whether this unfinished business may be adversely affecting your life. If so, describe how.

THE CRISIS OF MEANING

Before we consider some remedies for value-judging, let's reaffirm the idea that not all judging is "bad." Unless we appropriately assess and even judge the issues of our lives, we cannot progress in our quest for meaning.

Twentieth-century Supreme Court Justice Louis Brandeis said, "Sunlight is said to be the best of disinfectants...."[5] Brandeis was referring to the need to expose inequities in order to root them out of society. But the principle can also be applied to our personal lives, especially in regard to our destinies. Until we shine the sunlight of understanding on our individual identities, our destinies can remain mired in unrecognized deceptions.

To expose our thinking to the light, we need to establish the starting point of destiny, which is your calling. Your calling is written into your destiny code and therefore into the fabric of your life. You may be "called" to politics. If you are, you possess the basic inclinations and giftings needed to pursue a life of public service in the political realm.

Whatever your calling, it is first experienced as a *crisis of meaning*, a question or series of questions most often tied to your authentic identity and way of being. In Chapters One and Five, we touched on some of life's most fundamental questions:

- Who am I, really?

- Who am I in relation to others?

- Where am I headed, and why?

- What is the essential meaning of my life and how can I live my purpose...fully, joyfully, and without compromise?

We ask these questions because we seek the meaning of our lives. We have seen that when the need for meaning is unmet, we feel shallow, empty, useless, powerless, and inadequate. However, when we expose these questions to the "sunlight" of inquiry, we can begin to judge who we are and whether we are progressing toward our destinies.

Absent this process, we cannot become established in our identities to become the fulfilled, accomplished people we were created to be. Instead, we will grasp at momentary, expedient solutions to life's challenges. The crisis of meaning is instrumental in keeping us on course by delineating our priorities and helping us to maintain the organic connection between identity and destiny.

The Greek language supports this critical connection. The Greek word Κρίση is translated *crisis*. Its definition includes the concept of a "turning point."[6] The same word is also translated *judgment*. This definition includes the idea of "assessment."[7] Assessments and turning points are linked in life as they are in language.

The reason we experience crises of meaning is because we are born meaning makers. We are not prone to walking away from confusing ideas or circumstances without trying to iron them out. Crises of meaning inspire us; they cause us to seek answers and understanding. They propel us forward toward our destinies by prompting us to assess the correlation between our life experiences and our goals. Then, when our assessments reveal disparities, we are positioned to make the critical decisions that lead to positive turning points.

Do you remember Viktor Frankl's death camp experience discussed in Chapter Two? As he selected a coat from a heap of clothing stripped from those who had already been executed, Frankl found in the pocket a page torn from a Jewish prayer book. In the midst of utter senselessness, despair, and death, he was inspired to pursue an exemplary life governed by his beliefs. This turning point became an anchor for Frankl; it held him steady in the fierce waters of the Nazi concentration camps.[8]

Crises of meaning are powerful generators of "new" things. They produce innovations, fresh paradigms, and life improvements; they empower us to navigate seasons of transition; and they test our outcomes to ensure fulfillment of our potential.

THE VALUE-JUDGING ENGINE

The sound judgments we make benefit our development. It bears repeating that these are the well-founded, conscious evaluations or judgments we control. The judgments that occur in the unconscious realm are the ones we want to avoid. They are hidden from plain sight, yet they hold tremendous power to control us.

Becoming aware of negative unconscious tendencies is the first step toward overcoming them. Once we can identify the conflicted undercurrents that divide us from within, we negate their power. Then we can reestablish singleness of vision—a seamless harmony of thoughts, desires, behaviors, and outcomes.

A divided vision can be exposed by asking a simple question: *Are there areas in which I can't seem to get out of my own way?* For example: do you long for intimacy, transparency, trust, and spontaneity in your relationships, yet feel isolated within them? This kind of dichotomy could be a sign that your behavior is de-selecting the very outcomes you seek. (For more examples, see Figure 6.)

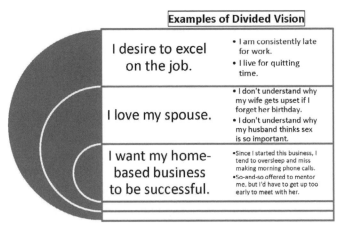

Figure 6

Since behavior can be hidden in emotional blind spots, we often have to discover areas of divided vision by examining visible, measurable outcomes. In the case of relational intimacy, you can evaluate your singleness of vision by probing the intimacy and authenticity demonstrated in your relationships. If your relational outcomes are incongruent with your desires, find out why. Consider this dichotomy to be an opportunity—a crisis of meaning capable of inducing self-examination and generating outcomes more consistent with your desires and destiny.

This kind of self-examination can help to expose the divisions that creep into the heart-mind connection. Often, the division involves a fundamental lack of acceptance—an unwillingness to take in stride the realities of life related to situations, people, and events. In the instance of our example regarding intimacy, failure to achieve that intimacy could indicate a failure to accept the fact that intimate relationships don't just happen; they require commitment, focus, and ongoing attention. This denial of reality could be tied to a value judgment that says: *If this were a destiny relationship, it would function effectively on auto-pilot.*

All of this value-judging occurs at the unconscious level and, unless it is resolved at the conscious level, it will continue to produce unwanted outcomes. Consider Sally. She and her boyfriend, Tim, recently broke up. Although their relationship started out on a high note, Tim says Sally began to henpeck him and became impossible to please. She was increasingly disapproving of his fashion choices and habitually embarrassed him in front of their friends.

Not surprisingly, Sally claimed that Tim was boorish and grew increasingly so as time went on. His apartment was a mess and his manners left her wanting. He failed to appreciate Sally's refined sensibilities and consistently embarrassed her in front of their friends.

Then Sally met Aaron. He was attractive, intelligent, and more refined than Tim. Sally was excited by the tenor of their new relationship: they were romantic, spontaneous, and in tune with each other. She was proud to show him off to her friends and loved hearing their comments about his excellent appearance. Relieved to have found the "right" guy, Sally's hopes for the relationship ran high.

For a time, things went well. Sally and Aaron became closer; their relationship grew more serious. Before long, however, Sally began to notice that Aaron had some irritating features she hadn't noticed at first: he threw his dirty socks on the floor of his apartment; he was nonchalant about his appearance when they were out of the public eye; and he had a tendency to crunch on ice cubes. Suddenly, Aaron began to look more like Tim. Fearing that she had met another loser, Sally bemoaned her disappointment to a friend and asked, "Why do I meet all the slobs?"

Of course, Tim and Aaron are human beings with issues of their own. But Sally's outcomes hint at an issue inscribed on her side of the ledger, a conflict between her relational desires and her expectations of the men in her life. Sally's dissatisfaction with yet another "boorish" man may indicate value judgments that leave her unable to accept the realities of human relationship.

At an unconscious level, Sally may believe that a "good" man does and sees everything the way she does. She may harbor the expectation that relationship is always pleasing and never challenging. Unless these value judgments are uncovered, the disconnection between Sally's head and heart will continue to control her outcomes. She will judge every man she meets to be a boor.

The Value-Judging Antidote

Relationship is part of the grand design of our lives. Our development, emotional growth, and success are fostered in the context of human interaction. Therefore, relationships are essential to unfolding destiny.

No one achieves destiny alone. Therefore, relational peace (which rests on a foundation of unconditional acceptance) is critical to our cause. This peace is only experienced to the degree that our vision is singular. As long as we are divided from within, torn between the conscious desires we readily acknowledge and the unconscious tendencies that operate out of sight, our ability to give and receive acceptance is compromised. The division tearing at our souls causes us to scrutinize rather than accept ourselves and others. The less acceptance-oriented we are, the more isolated, unhappy, and resistant to openness we become. As a result, our capacity for acceptance—however limited it might have been—contracts even more.

This capacity can be measured and increased. For example, the measure of your capacity to accept yourself unconditionally can be seen in the level of your acceptance of others. If you sit in judgment over others, you can be sure you raise the same scepter against yourself. In addition, your giving of acceptance to others determines the level of acceptance you receive from them. (You have to give acceptance to receive it.) The more open-hearted you are, the more productive this exchange becomes.

We know that part of this openness involves willing self-discovery. We also know how important it is to uncover any incongruent feelings lodged between the head and the heart. But we must also become aware of the degree to which we are invested in these incongruent feelings. Independent judgments run deep in the unconscious; they constitute a powerful but subliminal guidance system that controls our conduct. As long as judgments and other misperceptions are allowed to operate under the radar of the conscious mind, we will work unconsciously to protect them.

These feelings and thought patterns become fortified fixtures of our unfinished business—an uneasy comfort zone with which we are complicit. Upsetting this status quo is not easy; when we begin to identify and dislodge the emotional structures that have been erected over time, we tend to experience the turbulence and uncertainty that are common in seasons of change.

Unlike the disconnection that occurs between heart and mind, this kind of turbulence is a natural part of the destiny walk. If we are committed to achieving our destinies, we must look the unconscious in the eye, step outside our comfort zones, and release ourselves and others from value judgments—both the ones we harbor and the ones we have yet to formulate.

In doing so, we set ourselves free from the tyranny of an unrestrained unconscious mind...and from a past that has no right to claim the future.

ENDNOTES

1. Genesis 2:16-17 TM.

2. Genesis 3:1-13, paraphrased.

3. WorldofQuotes.com, http://www.worldofquotes.com/author/George-Eliot-(pseudonym-of-Mary-Ann-Evans-Cross)/1/index.html (accessed August 7, 2009).

4. Dr. Mark Chironna, *Stepping Into Greatness* (Lake Mary, FL: Charisma House, 1999), 67-68.

5. "Louis D. Brandeis Quotes," BrainyQuote, http://www.brainyquote.com/quotes/authors/l/louis_d_brandeis.html (accessed August 7, 2009).

6. *Babylon Translation @ a click*, s.v., "crisis," http://www.babylon.com/define/105/Greek-Dictionary.html (accessed August 7, 2009).

7. Ibid, s.v., "judgment," http://www.babylon.com/define/105/Greek-Dictionary.html (accessed August 7, 2009).

8. Anna Redsand, *Viktor Frankl: A Life Worth Living* (New York: Clarion Books, 2006), 70.

Unfold Your Destiny

1. Consider the nine value-judging behaviors described in this chapter. Are any of these behaviors apparent in your life? If so, consider the outcomes each behavior has produced. Are they consistent with your unfolding destiny? Explain.

   _____

   _____

   _____

   _____

   _____

   _____

   _____

2. Are you currently experiencing a crisis of meaning? What is the fruit of that crisis so far, and how might it prove to be a turning point in your life?

   _____

   _____

   _____

   _____

   _____

   _____

   _____

3. Becoming aware of negative unconscious tendencies is the first step toward overcoming them. Are you becoming aware of any unconscious tendencies in your life? What are they?

_____

_____

_____

_____

_____

_____

_____

_____

CHAPTER SEVEN

Freedom in Forgiveness

"Forgiveness is the fragrance that the violet
sheds on the heel that has crushed it."
—Mark Twain

A WEALTHY MAN HAD TWO sons. The younger had a restless streak. He asked for his share of the family inheritance and left home flush with cash, which he soon squandered. Impoverished and befallen by famine, the young man got a job feeding swine. Desperate for something to eat, he considered dipping into the slop the pigs seemed so happy to consume.

The irony of his situation struck the young man. "How many of my father's hired men have more than enough bread, but I am dying here with hunger!"[1] he exclaimed.

Humbled and heading for home, the prodigal hoped for little more than a meal and a menial job. Meanwhile his father kept vigil, always looking toward the horizon for his wayward son. One day, he spotted the prodigal off in the distance. Filled with compassion, he ran to the young man, embraced him, kissed him, and ordered a lavish celebratory meal to be prepared in his honor. Instead of giving him a meal and a job, the father restored his son's position in the family.

The biblical story of the prodigal son demonstrates the epitome of unconditional acceptance: it is the act of forgiveness. The young man made poor choices with commensurate consequences. He rejected his family, recklessly diminished a fortune he had not earned, and broke his father's heart. As awful as his offenses were, his father forgave him, without condition.

Offenses are a fact of life. Anyone who lives beyond the point of birth will be hurt by others, even by those closest to them. Some offenses are outright transgressions, as were the misdeeds of the prodigal son. Often, however, we take offense based not on an actual wrong committed but on something more ethereal—a value judgment we project from the unconscious onto others. These judgments can be revealed in the words we use to describe the offense:

- "He always finds a way to embarrass me in public."

- "She wore that dress to distract attention from my award celebration."

- "If you really loved me, you wouldn't hound me about overspending."

Not knowing the context in any of these cases, there is the possibility that the offended person's concern is legitimate. Often, however, such offenses are based in misperception. Whether umbrage is taken over real offenses or fabricated ones, they create the same dynamics: emotions are bruised; resentment festers; retaliation is considered; relationships are fractured. Whatever the source or category of offense may be—forgiveness is the answer (see Matt. 6:14 and 2 Cor. 2:7).

FORGIVENESS REALITY CHECK

In Chapter Six, I asked you to take a moment to identify hidden spots in which you carry anger and resentment. Notice, I did not ask *if* there was any anger or resentment. These emotions are facts of the human condition, and everyone deals with them.

If everyone experiences anger and resentment, it naturally follows that every one of us needs to forgive someone for something. This forgiveness is not a blanket denial of misdeeds. It is a willful decision that first acknowledges the impact of the wrong and then releases the offender from the burden of judgment. This choice has the added benefit of dissolving any unfinished business related to the offense and releasing the forgiver from a life of victimhood. It's easy to see why withholding forgiveness (even when the offender is dead wrong) would be counterproductive.

Forgiveness, of course, plays out in the realm of relationships, a key portion of our lives' grand design. If you cannot achieve destiny alone and relational peace is key to destiny fulfillment, then forgiveness is a non-negotiable element of destiny fulfillment. The corollary is this: as long as there is something left to forgive (an unresolved issue or offense), an obstacle remains lodged between you and your destiny.

Isolation is one such obstacle. You'll remember that value-judging separates us from others. We hand down many judgments to individuals; but we also declare judgment against groups and other segments of society. We consciously and unconsciously judge those who live in other neighborhoods; we declare verdicts against members of other political parties; we even point fingers and disrespect those whose religious or denominational beliefs differ from ours.

Judgments made on these broad levels contribute to factionalism. We dislike a system or organization; therefore we demean and even demonize its adherents, most of whom we don't know. This kind of value-judging is revealed by the same behaviors we discussed in the previous chapter. Figure 7 highlights value-judging earmarks in this broader context.

JUDGMENTS AND FACTIONALISM	
BEHAVIOR TYPE	STATED VALUE JUDGMENT
Criticism	All lawmakers are power-mongers.
Comparison	Members of my political party are more open-minded than folks in other parties.
Competition	Our goal is to surpass the membership roles of the church down the street.
Sarcasm	Our competitor's best ideas are stolen from us.
Mind Reading	The people in that "other department" won't be happy until our production numbers drop.

JUDGMENTS AND FACTIONALISM	
BEHAVIOR TYPE	STATED VALUE JUDGMENT
Assuming	Corporate bigwigs have hearts of stone. They don't give a fig for people.
Relational Stress	We gave opposing factions some seriously bad press at the convention. It caused plenty of drama, but we eventually had everyone eating out of our hands.
Projection	Rich people are ashamed of their money.
Labeling	Doctors are crooks and lawyers are ambulance chasers.

Figure 7

Often, the root of offense is found in the systems within which groups of people operate. These systems promote the behaviors we hold in disdain. Yet, instead of judging the system and forgiving the people, we judge the people and forgive the system. On the flip side, we ourselves become addicted to these systems. Because of our unfinished business, we attempt to inflate our self-esteem by participating in these systems (organizations, sectors, societal segments, etc.) and identifying with them. This is not to say that being a part of something bigger than us is inherently problematic. The problem arises when unmet needs drive us to extract affirmation from our affiliations.

When we are incongruent within ourselves, we tend to identify with systems for the wrong reasons. We also self-justify the value judgments we hand down by fabricating a framework in which we deem it acceptable (or even expected) to cut down those who don't act like us, talk like us, or achieve in the same ways we do.

To remain on the path of unfolding destiny, subject your affiliations and belief systems to scrutiny. Understand what draws you to certain affiliations. Know whether your reasons for being there are constructive. Become consciously aware of the degree to which you have melded yourself with a belief system that is functioning to your detriment or the detriment of others. Identify any evidence that you are value-judging others based on an unconscious agenda—and if you find evidence, be ready to forgive yourself and those you held in derision.

Finally, as regards both individual and broad value judgments, examine your thinking and behaviors with the goal of revealing any masks behind which you hide feelings of malice, division, and strife. Do you distrust those who belong to a certain denomination, yet put on airs of magnanimity in their presence? Are you working to create false impressions of good will or compassion? Determine to face those feelings without your self-protective gear. Become fully conscious of their existence and of the ways in which they manifest. Draw these unconscious value judgments out of hiding and expose them to the light of truth.

FORGIVENESS IS...

Forgiveness is nonnegotiable. It is the universal remedy for offense, anger, and resentment—a healing balm that releases offender and offended from the torment of untoward choices and outcomes. To borrow from Mark Twain, forgiveness is the fragrance that lingers in the heart long after the crushing blow of an offense has struck it.

Before we discuss what forgiveness is, let me first share a word of caution and a quick explanation of what forgiveness is not. The caution is against familiarity. Forgiveness is a familiar topic. We hear so much about it that we tend toward *reductionism*, the temptation to reduce the subject to fit what we already know about it. This response protects our hidden spots and prevents healing. It limits growth by assuming that we have mastered the issue at hand and have nothing more to learn about it or ourselves.

As for what forgiveness is not: it is not a feeling. If our ability to forgive were based on how we feel, we would forgive no one. Our pain and feelings of judgment, self-righteousness, and self-justification would forbid it. Instead, forgiveness is an act that supersedes our emotions and ultimately transforms them.

If forgiveness is not a feeling, then what is it? For the purposes of our discussion it is three things: a choice, a lifestyle, and a process.

Forgiveness Is a Choice

When an offense occurs, emotions are unleashed and mind-sets are uncovered. The offense triggers a series of responses that, left unchecked, will gain momentum and imprison us in its fury. To supersede this emotional ground swell and forgive requires a firm decision to resist its control.

Easy? No. Choosing to forgive, especially when you've been clearly wronged, goes against the grain of what seems to be just. It defies our human sensibilities and prompts us to dig below the ground of our natural abilities to seek the supernatural power to forgive. For me, as a pastor and believer in Jesus Christ, the grace to forgive without equivocating comes from Him.

The decision to resist the emotions triggered by an offense is a consequential one. It is a fundamental relational shift by which perspectives can be adjusted, defensive postures can be dropped, and compassion can override the temptation of revenge. All of these responses are counter-intuitive, emotionally speaking.

Forgiveness is, in fact, a choice we make in spite of our feelings. When we forgive, we declare our acceptance of those who are part of life's grand design; we acknowledge the fact that relationships work to "process" us for destiny fulfillment. We also yield to a new, albeit uncomfortable, context within which personal growth can flourish.

That growth is not guaranteed to be painless. In my own life, the process of acceptance required me to overcome a significant hurdle: my father's desire for me to be a medical doctor.

As a child, I accepted my dad's plan. If you asked me what I was going to be when I grew up, my answer would have been, "I'm going to be a doctor." Yet, a career in medicine was not *my* desire. It was an expectation I agreed to fulfill because I loved my dad and valued his approval.

Had I attempted to live my dad's dream, I would surely have failed. I might have been a good doctor, but at the expense of my authentic identity and life's purpose. Still, living my own dream would mean disappointing my dad, at least initially.

For my dad and me, coming to terms with our mis-matched goals produced opportunities for forgiveness and a measure of personal growth that, in retrospect, shows the painful parts of the process to be well worth the trouble.

Forgiveness Is a Lifestyle

We withhold forgiveness when we are bound by value-judging. These unconsciously held tenets of our worldview predispose us to certain habitual responses. Without realizing it, we pick and choose whom we will forgive or condemn—and under what circumstances.

Through the prism of our unconscious criteria, we decide who is worthy of our love and affection and who is deserving of rejection.

This pattern of value-judging can only be dismantled through a lifestyle of acceptance and forgiveness. We must consciously replace knee-jerk responses with interactions based in reality and truth. When we make the switch, we reap the ongoing benefits of an emotionally, socially, and even professionally enriched life.

Forgiveness Is a Process

Forgiveness is not an event. Nor is it a random act. Forgiveness is a process we are invited to enter. This process facilitates the healthy exploration of underlying issues that support value-judging. It also promotes the healing of past wounds and empowers us to assess future offense without the distortion of projection and other negative behaviors.

The lasting fruit of the process of forgiveness is an increase in relational peace and the removal of obstacles from the pathway of destiny.

Forgiveness Checkpoint

Forgiveness is not a feeling, but a choice and a lifestyle. Consider an experience in your life in which you experienced compassion for your offender *after* you made the choice to forgive.

NINE STEPS TO FORGIVENESS...AND FREEDOM

Value-judging and forgiveness go hand in hand. Demystify one and you dismantle the other.

Getting a handle on the issue of forgiveness is what natural-born meaning-makers crave. Armed with the meaning we need, we are empowered to navigate the troubled waters of offense. Conversely, as long as the process of forgiveness remains obscure, the pain we experience (and all of us experience pain in one area or another) will continue without relief.

With healing and restoration as our immediate goals, let's identify and undertake nine steps in the process of forgiveness.

1. Deal with denial.

Unforgiveness is pickled in denial. This denial occurs primarily on the unconscious level. When there is an altercation, we often deny our contributory role. When anger and resentment invade our relationships, we reject the reality that our value judgments poisoned the environment and predisposed the relationship to failure. Because our unfinished business creates emotional blind spots, our perspectives and memories are selective, causing us to self-justify and lay blame elsewhere. Denial becomes a permission slip to off-load the burden of wrongdoing and avoid the introspection that would dislodge comfortable, but harmful paradigms. Because denial occurs in the unconscious, it controls us and must be brought to our attention, both through prayerful introspection and the intervention of others.

When we face the truth, we are empowered to forgive.

2. Confront emotional pain.

Healthy confrontation is based on thoughts rather than feelings. Unfortunately, the emotions we want to confront don't think; they feel. Attempts to analyze our emotions end up exacerbating our frustrations because we gain little understanding. We confront our emotions, not by analyzing, but by reckoning with them—by exposing them and standing them up against the truth. This process produces tension, because deep down, we would rather not surrender our emotions, even if they are based in fallacy. Instead, we want to defend our right to be right. The choice on the path of unfolding destiny then becomes clear: *Do I want to be right or do I seek to be reconciled? How much destiny am I willing to exchange for winning an argument?*

When reconciliation is weighed against the need to be proven right, forgiveness becomes the clear choice.

3. Process your fear.

You cannot confront emotional pain without confronting the underlying fear. This is true of many emotions including grief, resentment, indignation, and anger (remember that anger is a mask for fear). Much of this processing can be done internally. For instance, when you become angry, you can pause and ask yourself *What am I afraid of in this situation?* Once you consciously make the anger-fear connection, you can confront the emotional root that is driving your reactions.

To experience lasting growth in this area, bring a significant other into the process. Choose someone caring and competent who will hold you accountable for your feelings and projections and help you to avoid the pitfalls of a victim mentality. This is not to say that we are never victimized. However, the victim mind-set is self-sabotaging. It convinces us that we are powerless and without choices. It places blame completely outside the realm of our control and beyond the range within which we can create change. It adds insult to injury; it promotes self-indulgence, whining, and stagnancy; it postpones healing; and it creates larger, more insidious wounds than our offenders could ever inflict.

When we refuse to conceal our fears and choose to process them instead, we become open to forgiveness.

4. Give and receive unconditional love.

Just as forgiveness is choice and not a feeling, unconditional love is a choice not necessarily supported by our feelings. Just as is true of affirmation and acceptance, we cannot give love if we are unwilling to receive it and we cannot receive the love we refuse to give. Here's a checklist that serves as a succinct reminder along the path of unfolding destiny:

- I cannot give what I do not have.
- I cannot have what I have not done.
- I cannot do what I have not been.
- I cannot be what I have not believed.
- I cannot believe what I have not received.
- I cannot receive what I have not been given.
- Therefore, I cannot give what I do not have.

Unconditional love, forgiveness, affirmation, and acceptance are choices made at a conscious level, often in spite of our feelings.

5. Realize that the only feelings you can control or create are your own.

Accept the reality that you and you alone are responsible for your feelings. Although others can commit offenses, they cannot produce or maintain your emotions. They cannot make or keep you happy, sad, or angry. When you feel hurt, it is important to realize this emotion is the residue of anger that has not been processed.

When we nurse our hurts we are hurting ourselves; we are holding onto anger and turning it inward. A better choice is to refuse victimhood, own our anger, regain our personal power, and bring a positive outcome out of the ashes of a seeming setback.

A word about denying and disconnecting from your anger: to do so requires that you deny and become detached from yourself. This is an unhealthy, untruthful choice that promotes the projection of your anger onto others and increases the likelihood of chronic mental and emotional disturbance. It is far better to face the facts and admit that your anger was your choice. This admission fosters the resolution of unfinished business. Here's a good rule of thumb: You cannot erase what you refuse to face.

Because no one is responsible for our feelings but us, we can forgive those who have failed to "make" us feel the way we long to feel.

6. Accept your part and release self-blame.

It takes two to tango, as the expression goes, and much of dance is hidden from view. Why? Because interactions are like icebergs; we see only the part that rises above the water line. Hidden from view is the largest part of the mass—in the case of interaction, the unconscious part of every exchange. If we deny the fact that we play a role in our negative interactions with others, we ignore our unconscious activity and give it license to control our lives.

That control is a high price to pay just to be excused from blame. It is not the only price, however. When we hold others accountable for the incongruities in our lives, we invite more negative outcomes. For example, if you suffer from the fear of rejection, but believe others are solely responsible for the rejection you experience, you are in denial. In overlooking your role, you inadvertently institutionalize the value judgments and projections that prompt others to reject (or appear to reject) you. Until the issue is confronted, you will habitually reject the parts of self that you dislike, in essence creating an enemy within. As long as the root of the problem remains intact, the same old issues will spring up in new situations.

A word about self-rejection: to avoid pain, we separate ourselves from the parts of self we dislike. At a fundamental level, our judgments against self create projection and dissociation. This state of consciousness (a *state* encompasses mood, belief, attitudes, and feelings) prevents healing and reinforces fragmentation. We become stuck in these states where all of our emotions become tangled. Therefore we bring to our relationships confusion, disorientation, and a lack of authentic intimacy.

Forgiveness is the switch that sheds light on our emotional webs and releases us from "stuck" states of consciousness.

7. See the offense as an opportunity for growth and enlargement.

When things go badly or events take a bad turn, we long to return to status of "the day before." Unfortunately, offenses cannot be undone. They can, however, be owned within the context of life's grand design. Instead of obsessing on the negative effects of an offense (as profound and unfair as these effects may be), allow the issue to bring forth something of value—find the silver lining and use it to your advantage. Viewed in a constructive light, every offense is an opportunity to grow.

When the growth aspect of forgiveness is fully recognized, forgiveness becomes second nature.

8. Establish accountability with someone you trust.

In Step 3 of the forgiveness process, we discussed accountability in the area of fear. Holding yourself accountable to an empathetic, objective, and supportive person is helpful in other areas of unfolding destiny. Ask this individual to hold up the mirror that will help you move away from blame games toward health and well-being. Receive this person's emotional support, but not at the expense of being told the truth. Use this person's feedback to help chip away at any self-protection mechanisms you have erected. This accountability and outside input will help you to live the lifestyle of forgiveness.

Practice and accountability promote the forgiveness lifestyle.

9. Release forgiveness through faith.

It takes faith to forgive instead of blame. This faith is a decision; it says, *"There is more to this than what I see. Doing what my emotions dictate will not produce the long-term results I truly desire."*

Choose to forgive no matter the cost of the offense. Avoid the trap of ongoing passive-aggressive acts of retaliation. Release the offender from the virtual prison cell he or she "deserves" to occupy and release yourself into your destiny. Decide that your freedom is greater recompense than any payback you could extract and your destiny is more valuable than being right.

Forgiveness may be counterintuitive; but unforgiveness is counterproductive.

Keep this blueprint for the forgiveness process handy and put it to work for you! Next—the seven secrets!

ENDNOTE

1. Luke 15:17.

UNFOLD YOUR DESTINY

1. Can you remember a specific occasion on which some-
    one forgave you when you least expected it? Describe
    the experience and what you learned through it.

    _____

    _____

    _____

2. Can you identify a person whom you need to forgive for
    an offense (spoken or unspoken) that has caused great
    pain? How do you feel about forgiving this individual?
    What do you think will happen when you forgive?

    _____

    _____

    _____

3. Are you withholding forgiveness from yourself for an
    offense you have committed? Will you offer yourself
    the unconditional acceptance you hope to give and
    receive from others?

    _____

    _____

    _____

PART
III

UNPACK THE SECRETS

(How to Unfold Destiny Daily)

Chapter Eight

Unfolding Destiny: Secrets 1 & 2

*"Before everything else,
getting ready is the secret of success."*
—Henry Ford

Y OU ARE READY, AND it's time to move forward! You are
aware of the workings of the unconscious mind. You have
tackled the fundamental issues of destiny, identity, esteem, values,
affirmation, and more. You are a card-carrying, conscious meaning-
maker who understands the workings of acceptance and the lifestyle
of forgiveness. You have packed your bags for unfolding destiny and

have divested of unfinished business. You are ready to run the ball downfield. So put on your cleats and prepare to receive the pass. The Seven Secrets of Unfolding Destiny will take you into the end zone!

SECRET 1
Destiny Unfolds as Crisis and Process

"Every crisis is an opportunity."

"Life is a process."

These are common statements in the modern lexicon. Their use is so widespread, we tend to slough them off as clichés. But here's another adage: Clichés develop for a reason, and that reason is common experience.

We have already searched out the concepts of crisis and process with a noncynical eye. We have talked about crises of meaning and the processes involved in creativity, discovery, being and becoming, forgiveness, and unfolding destiny. In our discussions, we learned that crises really do create opportunities for growth. We have also seen how the willingness to engage in life's processes helps to produce an inner congruence between the desire for destiny fulfillment and the fully conscious commitment to achieve it.

In Chapter Seven, we touched on the topic of familiarity. It is no secret that, on a visceral level, we equate familiarity with comfort, predictability, and security. If you are lost on a dark, unfamiliar road, a familiar sight is reassuring. It helps you put a fix on your location and lends welcome predictability to the remainder of the trip. Feeling secure, confident, and at ease, you can lean back and turn up the road music.

Familiarity has its upside—and its downside. Ensconced in the familiar, we are tempted to resist the very changes that are part of unfolding destiny. We can become so familiar in our relationships that we begin to overlook the value of others: we take loved ones for granted; we focus on their weaknesses instead of their strengths; we assume that their needs are met and that they "know what we mean" when we speak (and even when we fail to express what they need to hear).

Perhaps our weakness for familiarity is part of the reason that destiny must unfold as crisis and process. For certain, destiny cannot be achieved from the comfort zone. It requires an active, ongoing, vibrant pursuit—the kind that is rarely conducted from the sofa with a remote control and a bag of chips.

The mere utterance of the word *crisis* implies an unfolding of events that defies our plans and preferences. Yet, the word needn't make us cringe. If we will drop our value judgments and look at crisis from a renewed, truth-based perspective, we will remember that crises work for us when we let them. If we embrace crises, they cause us to crave our destinies even more.

Point taken: Destiny unfolds as crisis and process. On a practical level, when you embrace a crisis, you activate it (more about this later). An activated process implies the absence of inertia and the presence of motion. For the process to remain active, we must interact with it. Once the switch is flipped, you can expect to leave the doldrums. At times, you will feel as though you were being shot out of a cannon. That's OK; it's part of the destiny walk. Choose to get in the flow and go with it.

It's your life; engage it!

THE FREEDOM OF NOT KNOWING

Remember the Adam and Eve lesson: there is a certain amount of freedom in not knowing it all. When we still have things to learn, we don't view the world through a "ho-hum" lens of familiarity. Instead, we become more curious, alert, and teachable.

Familiarity inhibits inquisitiveness. If you assume that you have been there and done that, you will also assume that the knowledge you have is all that's available. Without knowing it, you will have inscribed a virtual box around the body of your knowledge and experience and buried it in the deep soil of presumption.

We naturally develop an unspoken loyalty to the status quo— what we know and think we know about the world—and we unconsciously protect it. But, for destiny to unfold in all its glory, we must be willing *not* to know it all and commit to the path anyway.

There needs to be an intentional flexibility in the heart of the destiny achiever that allows for an unfolding of things bigger than imagined. This elasticity of thought and perspective makes room for us to know things we have never known before. These new things include fresh ideas; new realms of success, fulfillment, and contribution; innovative approaches to "old" challenges; increased freedom to give and receive love, acceptance, and affirmation; renewed perspectives regarding capability and capacity to achieve; new views of what is possible.

The willingness to *not* know everything ahead of time gives us the freedom to pursue our "biggest" destiny. Instead of trying to force our finite, often self-limiting expectations to become reality, we remain open to the really big things we could never have imagined possible.

We *allow* ourselves to enter the destiny stream already prepared for us.

CRISIS AS A GIFT

Crisis is a facet in the gem of unfolding destiny. It is part of destiny's grand design. The crisis of meaning is designed to convey you along a productive, well-placed path into an emotional, cognitive, and spiritual environment conducive to destiny fulfillment. But first, you must be willing to embrace the crisis as a gift.

When you embrace this place of necessary discomfort and unease, the specific process suited to your life's purpose at that moment is activated. No longer will you question the whys, hows, and wherefores of the crisis. No longer will you wonder whether the crisis resulted from something that was done right or something that went horribly wrong. Instead, you will focus on what to make of the crisis and how to effectively harvest its best fruit.

Crises of meaning are rarely convenient. They cause us to chafe and even tempt us to quit. Caught in the navel-gazing that often accompanies these arresting developments, we tend to trim our sails and narrow our focus. We conserve our energy and resources and try to "manage" the crisis. Almost instinctively, we scale down our dreams and wait for the storm to blow over.

Although these reflexes are second nature, they are unhelpful. They spring from the unconscious mind and its well-protected fears to produce a reactionary posture. We feel that we are acting prudently, but our reasons for withdrawing cannot be accurately assessed until they are lifted to the level of the conscious mind and tested by truth. Rationalizations come to our defense; we reason that we are attending to the urgent, but fail to notice that we are neglecting the larger context within which the crisis occurs.

Because we see crises as unwanted intrusions, protect against them. Henry Kissinger framed the sentiment in a humorous but perceptive one-liner, saying, "There can't be a crisis next week. My schedule is already full."[1] The sentiment is understandable, but if destiny unfolds as crisis and process, crises are written into our schedules. They do not interrupt life; instead, they are part of the grand design by which destiny is achieved.

Every process has multiple purposes. One process could be the means by which an item of unfinished business is healed and the method that settles the issue of your life's calling. It might even be the process by which you come to recognize your unique tendencies and abilities—and through which you meet a significant someone of influence and access in your field.

Invariably, the process moves more than one person closer to destiny fulfillment.

PROGRESS IN YOUR PROCESS

Every process unfolds incrementally in response to your engagement with it. The stages of the process are progressive; each one is conditioned on the one before it, as Figure 8 shows.

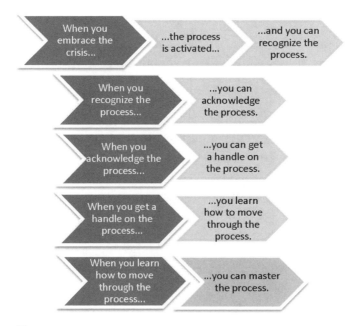

When you embrace the crisis... ...the process is activated... ...and you can recognize the process.

When you recognize the process... ...you can acknowledge the process.

When you acknowledge the process... ...you can get a handle on the process.

When you get a handle on the process... ...you learn how to move through the process.

When you learn how to move through the process... ...you can master the process.

Figure 8

Let's explore more fully your role in the process:

Embrace the Crisis

As mentioned earlier, this is where your involvement begins. When a crisis of meaning presents itself, you can choose to embrace it or you can run from it. Needless to say, if you choose the latter, you will face the challenges and issues later, in one form or another; and you will accumulate more unfinished business in the meantime.

Activate the Process

Embracing the crisis is productive and enriching. When you embrace the crisis, you automatically activate a process designed to accomplish something significant in your life. The instant the process wire is tripped, the clock starts running. The process has been unleashed, destiny is unfolding, and another level of engagement is required.

Recognize the Process

Once you have activated the process, you are able to consciously recognize it and make meaning of the experience. This is not the same as watching it happen; recognition involves actively seeking to understand what is going on. Until your desire to understand becomes a decision to do so, you are a bystander instead of an active participant in your unfolding destiny.

Acknowledge the Process

The process is dynamic. Once you recognize the process, you can acknowledge it. You are ready to make room for it, get in stride with it, appreciate the forward motion it provides, and discern the benefits that can result.

Get a Handle on the Process

That's when you begin to roll up your shirtsleeves and dig into the process by interacting with it on a practical level. Instead of seeing the process as a hodge-podge of disparate and demanding circumstances to be avoided, you see it as an environment in which to achieve particular destiny objectives. No longer are you under the control of the crisis; instead you've got a handle on the process and are working your God-given purposes through it.

Learn How to Move Through the Process

With a firm grip on the process, you are empowered to become proficient in it. You're in the destiny swing of things and you are moving through the process. It is *your* environment. You've taken ownership of it and will glean from it everything it has to offer. You don't allow the cost of the process (the discomforts, unknowns, or seeming setbacks) to arrest your development; you use the process to smooth your rough edges, hone your skills, and enlarge your capacity for transformation. Instead of being tossed by the waves, you ride them into destiny's shores!

Master the Process

As you move through the process, you learn the ropes. Unknowns become conquered territory. The place of unease becomes the petri dish of possibility. Fear gives way to the fierceness of purpose-filled desire. Efforts become more streamlined. Thoughts are focused in the right place at the right time for the right reasons. As you move through the process, you begin to master it.

When you perceive the process in light of your purpose and consciously engage with it, mastery is assured—and destiny unfolds.

Secret 1 Checkpoint

Identify any crisis and process you are currently experiencing. Based on the steps described above, locate where you are in the process.

SECRET 2
NEITHER THE CRISIS NOR THE PROCESS ARE RANDOM

Nothing about your life is random. There are no crises or processes that occur as pure happenstance.

The unfolding of destiny springs from the orchestrated design of your life. Just as you are "endowed by [your] Creator with certain unalienable Rights,"[2] you are equipped by your Creator to execute an orchestrated design. No wonder your identity and destiny are inseparable! Your being leads to your doing and both operate in ways that cannot be duplicated by anyone else.

In Chapter Two, we poked around for clues to your identity and therefore your destiny. The indicators we sought were found in the simple facts of your life. They include these five:

1. Serendipitous moments you know amount to something more than mere coincidence.

2. Particular relationships that seem to be leading in a meaningful direction. Some of these relationships involve trusted friends, mentors, or family members who encourage you in specific pursuits or talents.

3. Particular activities that make time fly and leave you feeling fulfilled.

4. Your particular flair for doing things; the gifts you have that cause others to solicit your help, advice, or expertise.

5. The things you dream of doing "someday."

This list is not exhaustive, but serves as an apt reminder of the specificity that surrounds your existence, as encoded in your destiny DNA.

You'll recall that your destiny code is the road map to your "Promised Land." It delineates fine points that distinguish you from everyone else on the planet. When your destiny code is uncovered, it provides context for the past experiences you already understand and the ones that are still inscrutable on the cognitive level. This code serves as a blueprint for your future, a detailed accounting of the talents, strengths, proclivities, passions, relationships, and everything else that supports the fulfillment of your destiny.

Written into your destiny code are crises of meaning and the processes designed to resolve them. They are not designed to break you, but to build you up. Just as boot camp prepares a soldier for combat, these crises serve to develop your strengths, resolve inner conflicts and clarify objectives, identify areas of weakness, fortify your resolve, instill a sense of readiness, test your mettle, and increase your self-confidence.

Through these crises, your need for meaning is met. It is in the midst of them that life's most profound questions are answered. Unexpected circumstances drive you to dig deeper and reevaluate long-held perspectives. In crises, you find out what you are made of and you discover why you were created. You become familiar with your role and your place in the world. You discover your sphere of influence and the arenas to which you are called.

Over time, you realize that every crisis of meaning and every process it triggers runs parallel to the others. It becomes clear that, although they arrived unexpectedly, nothing about them is random.

THE PROCESS REFINES

Destiny fulfillment does not depend on the perfect expression of your best qualities. If it were, no human being could achieve it. Instead, it is dependent upon crisis and process and the purposeful refinement they instigate.

When a crisis of meaning is embraced and the process is activated, you will discover your weak points and the areas of distraction that dampen your effectiveness. This refining "fire" is part of the grand design. It clarifies your perspective by integrating what is within and what is "out there." As the fire grows hotter (and it will!) flecks of unfinished business or dross will surface and be separated from the pure molten material of your life. It is in this crucible that errant thoughts, misconceptions, and biases are strained out of your belief system. Attitudes are examined. Values are defined. Desires are scrutinized. Unfinished business is reconciled and released.

Tenacity, commitment, desire, passion, focus, authenticity—all are tested in the process. The trial replaces deception with truth and incongruities with harmonious thoughts, choices, and actions. It is the place where anger, resentment, self-pity, fear and intimidation, insecurities, self-hatred, and distorted expectations are pulled up by the roots so that the soil of your efforts can produce the destiny harvest you were created to yield.

YOUR FUTURE IS CALLING

Destiny codes link past, present, and future in a meaningful context. Discovery of your destiny "genes" brings a once obscure big picture into perspective. Suddenly, from the place called *today* you can peer into the past with more understanding and less angst. And, from the shores of today you can peer into the vision called *tomorrow*, not in fear and confusion, but with enthusiasm and conviction.

No matter where you stand in your progress toward destiny fulfillment, you can live with this vision in your mind and heart, knowing that it existed even before you knew it was there. You will hear the future calling when you see a toddler playing doctor, or a candidate enrolling in the police academy. You will hear your future calling every time your dream speaks to your heart about what can be.

At any given moment, you are processing or acting on information developed in the past from lessons learned, revelations received, disappointments digested, realizations made of unique talents and abilities. As you bring these data into the present via your thoughts, they interact with your vision of the future to produce new thoughts.

However bright, faint, or faded that vision may be, it contains all elements of destiny potential. When you grasp the enormity of this truth, your awareness becomes an engine capable of bringing these elements to combustion. Suddenly, your thoughts, desires, choices, actions, and dreams work together to generate destiny momentum.

If you will keep setbacks, disappointments, discouragement, and even failures in perspective, this momentum will help to carry you forward. You will be able to keep the picture of the future posted in your conscious mind. This is important, because the longer it remains in your "active file," the stronger the vision will become (and the more powerful your forward momentum). With each day of conscious pursuit, you will become bolder in your exploits and more determined to achieve your goals.

With every goal you meet, the fragrance of unfolding destiny will become more intense and alluring. That fragrance will beckon and draw you forward on the path. Hope for the future will enfold you until your hope is fulfilled and the expression of your purpose is in full bloom.

> ### Secret 2 Checkpoint
>
> Consider some of the most memorable, yet seemingly random experiences of your life. As you examine them from your current vantage point, can you identify a destiny "thread" tying them together? Explain.

Writer and philosopher William Hazlitt (1778-1830) wrote, "Books let us into their souls and lay open to us the secrets of our own."[3] The secrets I am sharing with you are not secrets to be kept, but to be shared. Like books, they serve not only to instruct and assist us along our destiny paths; they serve also to make us aware of the musings and motives of our own hearts.

That is part of the process. It is one of the ways in which the human need for meaning is met. As we discover all we were built to accomplish, we can't help but reflect on the desires, dreams, and visions incubating within us. Best of all, we learn that all of it is woven into a single bolt of cloth—the lush fabric of unfolding destiny!

ENDNOTES

1. "Henry A. Kissinger Quotes," BrainyQuote, http://www.brainyquote.com/quotes/quotes/h/henryakis101648.html (accessed August 23, 2009).

2. "The Declaration of Independence," The Charters of Freedom, The National Archives, http://www.archives. gov/exhibits/charters/declaration_transcript.html (accessed August 23, 2009).

3. "William Hazlitt Quotes," BrainyQuote, http://www. brainyquote.com/quotes/authors/w/william_hazlitt.h tm (accessed August 23, 2009).

UNFOLD YOUR DESTINY

1. As you study the seven secrets, keep your journal close by. Jot down the thoughts that come to mind, even those that seem inconsequential or unrelated to the topic of the moment. Commit to being a meaning-maker where these thoughts are concerned.

2. Make special note of any "lightning bolts" that strike as you study the secrets. Also make note of any distinct changes in your mind-sets or perspectives.

3. Consider how your writings in response to 1 and 2 might relate to your unfolding destiny. Where do they fit, and which dots do they help connect?

CHAPTER NINE

Unfolding Destiny: Secrets 3 & 4

Every day you may make progress.
Every step may be fruitful. Yet there will stretch out
before you an ever-lengthening,
ever-ascending, ever-improving path.
You know you will never get to the end of the journey.
But this, so far from discouraging,
only adds to the joy and glory of the climb.
—Sir Winston Churchill[1]

THE JOURNEY, WHAT WE will call the conscious march toward destiny, was epitomized in the life of Sir Winston Churchill. He remains a quintessential example of persistence, a man for whom soaring victories were sandwiched between great disappointments. Despite the mixed blessings along his path, Churchill was a man whose life and destiny were harmonized.

Churchill was familiar with crisis and mastered the process. His experiences and meaningful "coincidences" caused him to plumb the depths within himself and rise to destiny occasions, not only on the personal level, but on the international stage. So replete with influence and impact was his role that it would be impossible to understand 20th century history without recognizing Churchill's part in it.

Your potential is no less than Churchill's. Destiny is written into your DNA just as it was written into his. As we continue through the seven secrets, you will find more keys with which to unlock that potential. If you are ready for a gold mine of insights into the deeper workings of destiny achievement, secrets 3 and 4 are for you!

SECRET 3
THE DEPTHS WITHIN YOU ARE PROCESSED TO PROMOTE PROGRESS

Destiny requires that we be willing to engage the process and be processed ourselves. There is an openness of heart—a brokenness—possessed by those who fulfill their potential in life; it is a submission to reality and truth that allows for personal development at a high level.

This brokenness amounts to a relinquishment of your demands for a particular outcome in favor of the best outcome. For example, if your destiny is in medical missions, but a misplaced desire for a lavish lifestyle drives you to "settle" for a specialty practice in a posh neighborhood, you have chosen a particular outcome (which appears to be more rewarding on its face) over the best outcome (which would have proven to be more fulfilling in the end).

Brokenness releases the need to be right so that truth can be accurately perceived and genuine progress can be made. It amounts to a willful disentanglement and disengagement from the known, the comfortable, the self-centered requirements of ease and predictability. Brokenness can be seen as a willingness to let go, to release what you clutch most tightly so you can grasp something bigger.

Brokenness is the key to becoming and remaining unstuck in your endeavors. It opens your heart to new learning, enhanced awareness, exploration, discovery, hunger, curiosity, and yieldedness. It ensures your ability to take the progressive steps necessary to achieve your goals and it promotes clarity of vision, the ability to "see" where you are going.

EMOTIONS, THINKING, BEHAVIORS, AND ATTITUDES SOMETIMES ACCOMPANYING BROKENNESS
Weeping
Mourning
Sighing
Longing
Recognition of a lack or loss of vision
Recognition of an inability to take the next easiest step
A willingness to make a profound change from the inside out
The sensing of the call to "be and become"

Figure 9

THREE FUNDAMENTAL SHIFTS

In Chapter Seven, we talked about the fundamental relational shift that occurs when we choose to forgive rather than harbor an offense. This shift allows us to adjust our perspectives, drop our defensive postures, offer compassion, and resist revenge.

We learned that, on an emotional level, these responses are counterintuitive. The same dynamics surround brokenness. They empower us to relinquish control of our destinies and choose openheartedness instead. These simple choices are game changers that produce three fundamental shifts:

1. You see the world differently than you did before you "let go."

Until you allow your innermost depths to be processed, you will tend to seek safety from the world outside your window, not realizing that the fears you carry are not "out there" but inside of you.

When you allow your depths to be processed, you will begin to see the world as a wide-open space that is alive with possibilities—for you! You will begin to recognize opportunities and be empowered to actualize them.

When I embraced the fact that a career in medicine was not my destiny, I had to let go of the fear that my father would be disappointed in me. By facing this fear, I became willing to accept the consequences of my choices; I came to grips with the fact that I could not control my father's reaction to my decision and I accepted the fact that I might lose his emotional support.

The potential for loss was real, but what I gained was far more consequential: the wide-open road to my destiny! Instead of the narrow, constraining path dictated by the need for approval, I began a lifelong walk in the field of my dreams, a place where I could be myself, fulfill my life's purpose, and be a better son to my father in the long run.

In the final analysis, I chose my values over my needs. The process required of me a child*like* transparency to acknowledge my neediness so that I could relinquish my child*ish* need to be affirmed at all cost.

Still, it is easy to understand why so many people make the opposite choice. Emotional needs can exert tremendous power over our decisions. The medical missionary who chose the posh practice never faced that pressure head-on and therefore became unconsciously driven by it. Instead of taking an honest, childlike approach to unmet needs, the doctor remained enslaved to them.

When you deal squarely with your needs, you are free to be driven by your values instead. This level of maturity is one way in which we move through and master the process. In the final analysis, maturity enables you to influence the world at a level commensurate with your destiny capacity.

2. You see that all things in your life and experience are connected.

As you let go of your preconceived notions, you begin to see that your life is not a "rag rug" of swatches thrown together in a random pattern, but a fine cloth woven from many seemingly diverse threads. Every thread has its purpose and therefore its meaning. To attempt to disengage a particular thread from the weave would damage the cloth and defeat its overall purpose.

When you feel perplexed and uncertain about how a particular thread fits into the overall pattern of life, recalibrate your focus. Consider life's bigger picture. Remember that you were created by God with a purpose. That purpose is what gives meaning to your life in all its aspects. The threads that seem to be pulling away from the cloth of your life are actually working together to form a grand design.

When inner conflicts and incongruences arise, challenge them! The fullness of your destiny will become more evident as you do.

3. You come to cultivate a new way of listening.

When you allow yourself to let go and move forward, you inevitably find that your hearing must become more selective. Instead of feeding on the opinions of others, the worldview of media, the societal tugs to achieve or behave in ways that undermine destiny, you begin to listen the same way you are seeking to live—from the inside out. You learn to tune out the voices of fear, pain, frustration, dissatisfaction. Instead, you tune in the voices of truth that guide you in the direction of freedom, empowerment, encouragement, and a new brand of commitment to unfolding destiny.

The brokenness that produces these fundamental shifts produces other lasting effects, including a new level of integrity, in part because you are values-driven rather than needs-driven. You'll remember that when your values, needs, and wants are aligned, you are unlikely to make compromising choices or to suffer the inner turmoil these choices produce. Brokenness also yields a healthy move away from the fabrications of self-image and toward the experience of genuine esteem.

The brokenness, integrity, and authentic identity that result from the crisis of meaning (and the process that ensues) are the beginning of unfolding destiny.

Secret 3 Checkpoint

Consider areas in life in which you exhibit a sense of brokenness. Are there any other areas in which you feel that you are resisting it?

SECRET 4
SYNCHRONICITY MARKS YOUR MARCH TOWARD DESTINY

Unfolding destiny involves what I call the path of synchronicity, the place where destiny connections are made. These connections are instrumental, but never accidental. Instead, they are meaningful, even when mistaken for coincidence. The experiences that occur on the path of synchronicity have the potential, if they are recognized, to be life changing.

Synchronicity involves matters of time and timing. Events that are *synchronous* are "happening, existing, or arising, at precisely the same time."[1] The Greek root *chronos*, means "time."[2] This is physical time, a commodity of which we seem never to have enough. Because physical time is limited, it is anxiety-producing. This anxiety is often connected to esteem and performance issues and, as such, tends to diminish our creative and other capacities. Anxiety is mentally draining and blocks the free flow of intelligence. We become driven by fear and disconnected from our intuitive abilities.

You can see that chronos is an unforgiving taskmaster. The path of synchronicity is marked by a different kind of time described by the Greek word *kairos*. Rather than strict physical time, kairos can be described as "present-moment awareness time." It amounts to the suspension of time that is anxiety-driven and the ushering in of eternity-driven moments. Strong's Dictionary of Greek Words defines *kairos* as "an occasion, *i.e.* [the] set or proper time"[3] for something. It includes the idea of "opportunity… [the] (convenient [or] due) season"[4] in which a meaningful event occurs.

Anxiety in Action

"Anxiety is a 'fusing together' of feelings, memories, thoughts and speculations that are so tangled that we don't want to take the time to sort them out."[5] Left unresolved, anxiety produces and exacerbates the feeling of being "stuck," emotionally and otherwise.

Kairos time is pregnant with meaning that extends beyond the physical realm. It is the point in a crisis at which a defining moment becomes evident and the confluence of seemingly unconnected circumstances is yielding intricately designed results. In these moments, we become acutely aware that our destinies are far bigger than we know. This becomes evident in part because, in the kairos moment, meaningful coincidences that could not have occurred before now transpire effortlessly.

All of us have experienced kairos moments. Have you ever thought of someone who had long been out of sight and even mind, only to have them call you unexpectedly? Perhaps you have desired the opportunity to meet and learn from a particular leader in your field, someone you do not know personally and to whom you have no access. Suddenly, a friend invites you to dinner and announces that this leader will be joining you!

These examples of synchronicity are not only exciting, they are a form of provision for your destiny fulfillment. The educational and relational value of an arranged meeting with a prominent figure in your field of endeavor can provide something you could not get on your own: you could not beg for it, buy it, or steal it. These resources arrive at the appropriate time and were previously concealed from view. Often, they are resources that have lain dormant within you, but suddenly bubble to the surface where they can be developed and applied to the need of the moment.

When meaningful coincidences like this occur, they yield immeasurable value. This is provision of a high order.

KAIROS TIMING

The fourth secret of unfolding destiny is recognized and freely experienced once you have embraced the first three secrets. You have already grasped the fact that unfolding destiny is the product of crisis and process. You are cognizant of the fact that neither crisis nor process nor any other aspect of unfolding destiny occurs randomly. This awareness causes you to pay attention and give appropriate regard to your experiences. Because you realize that the depths within must be processed for you to experience genuine, steady progress, you become open-hearted and able to interact with the process you are in and receive from it.

Synchronicity is unleashed when you embrace the secrets. Yet, it often occurs in your moments of greatest frustration and despair. When you are at the end of your rope (and the end of yourself) and about ready to quit…when your resources are exhausted along with your understanding—that's when synchronicity kicks into high gear. This phenomenon is related to brokenness and the openness that it fosters.

Just when you have done all you can and all you know to do, another piece of your destiny puzzle falls into place, *miraculously!*

Secret 4 Checkpoint

Describe your most recent synchronicity experience. What did it provide?

KAIROS EFFECTS

Meaningful coincidences are productive events along the destiny path and serve as indicators of your progress in relation to your goals and calling. These events provide needed information in seven specific ways:

1. They "locate" you.

Experiences with synchronicity help you to understand where you are in the process of unfolding destiny. Consider our example of the unexpected dinner invitation: the timing of the meeting is not random; therefore the mere fact of the meeting's arrangement indicates that the groundwork for that meeting has already been laid. You are at the place in your destiny walk where you now need and are ready to receive what this individual has to offer. That helps to define exactly where you are.

2. They activate your passion.

If you are starting a software company and are invited to dinner with Bill Gates, your passion will ramp up. You know you are coming to a juncture that is stacked with meaning and potential; this affirms your sense of destiny and motivates you to dream big.

3. They solidify your purpose.

Meaningful coincidences add "meat" to the "bones" of your vision. They serve to reassure you that your purpose is not only valid, but important (worthy of your focus and worthy of the attention of others).

4. They energize your desires.

Imagine that you are a struggling actor who gets an audition with Steven Spielberg. Suddenly, you can taste what you have desired for so long. What has always been out of reach seems within your grasp. Your emotions attach to the possibilities and rekindle your desires in fresh ways.

5. They clarify your values.

Meaningful coincidences help you to refocus on what is most important to you. You are reminded of why you dream of being a doctor…a writer…a preacher…a fireman. The pursuit is based on the values that drove you in the first place. Kairos moments bring those values to the forefront anew.

6. They analyze your behaviors.

Kairos moments are always consequential. Whether they sooth or stretch you (and particularly if they stretch you) you will acquire a heightened awareness of what makes you tick. You will learn why you respond or fail to respond in certain ways at certain times. Meaningful coincidences will also highlight aspects of your way of being.

7. They amplify your future.

Meaningful occurrences have a way of enlarging the vision you carry in your mind and heart. The future becomes less obscure and more knowable. It moves from the background of your life (the "someday" syndrome) to the foreground of your life (an environment you can imagine entering).

When you enter the territory of Secret 4, you are a sharp, well-balanced arrow in the quiver of a masterful marksman. You are pointed directly at the target and will not be distracted. You recognize the need for clear boundaries that dictate the objects of your attention and you cast off distractions with the quick flick of a focused mind.

You grasp the fact that you have a destiny mission and you choose not to be deterred.

ENDNOTES

1. http://www.quotationspage.com/quote/2755.html.

2. "Synchronous," Merriam-Webster Online, *Merriam-Webster Online Dictionary* (2009), http://www.merriam-webster.com/dictionary/synchronous (accessed August 23, 2009).

3. *Babylon Translation @ a click*, s.v., "crisis," http://www.babylon.com/define/105/Greek-Dictionary.html (accessed August 7, 2009).

4. James Strong, *The Comprehensive Concordance of the Bible Together With Dictionaries of the Hebrew and Greek Words of the Original With References to the English Words* (Iowa Falls: World Bible Publishers), s.v. "kairos."

5. Ibid.

6. Dr. Mark Chironna, *Stepping Into Greatness* (Lake Mary, FL: Charisma House, 1999), 103.

UNFOLD YOUR DESTINY

1. You can probably identify a process already underway in your life. Can you identify ways in which you are allowing your own depths to be processed? If so, what progress is evident?

2. With which are you most familiar: chronos time or kairos time? Explain.

3. On a scale of one to five (five being "optimal"), how would you rate your ability to recognize and make the most of a meaningful coincidence? Give an example and explain ways you can heighten your awareness.

CHAPTER TEN

Unfolding Destiny: Secrets 5, 6, & 7

"The real voyage of discovery consists not in seeking new landscapes but in having new eyes."
—Marcel Proust

YOUR DESTINY CODE HAS been there all along. Once you discover it, it commands your attention. It focuses your vision in new ways; you could say that it gives you "new eyes," a pair of destiny lenses that see the world in a new and inviting way.

With those lenses firmly in place, the "old bets" are off: the limits on your potential are lifted; fear-based assumptions are dismantled; your dreams are taken down from the shelf and dusted off.

As you learn and implement the remaining secrets, your life will be infused with new vigor—not an incessant striving to make your life work, but an unstoppable energy that is fueled by knowing who you truly are and why you are here.

SECRET 5
YOUR DESTINY PATH BECOMES SELF-EVIDENT

In the box-office smash, *Raiders of the Lost Ark*, Indiana Jones faces a chasm that stands between him and the sacred cup. The gulf is so deep and the way so impossible that death is the only conceivable outcome. Even so, Jones will not surrender his quest. He takes a literal leap of faith and discovers a landing place that was not visible the moment before. Until he takes the leap, the pathway doesn't show up.

This is the precise experience of destiny achievers. Great gorges are wedged between them and their divine purposes—chasms that would intimidate the faint of heart and send them home convinced that defeat was the only possible outcome. But defeat is never the only available choice; destiny-minded people have learned that truth and are willing to prove it time after time, regardless of the chasm's dimensions.

Armed with a commitment to achieve your destiny, you can stand on the ledge of uncertainty and take the plunge. When you do, the next step of your path will be uncovered and you will march forward. This self-evident path will foster the confidence that you are on the right road. You will make the bold moves you feared in the past. Call it walking on water, stepping out of the boat, or taking a leap of faith, you will now recognize these moments when they come.

Because you are absorbed in a meaningful, fulfilling activity, your sense of chronos time will be lost along with the anxiety it once produced. You will feel yourself moving intuitively, as though guided by an internal treasure map in which you have the utmost confidence. You will become aware of a level of coordination that you've never known before, a working together of circumstances and relationships that you could not have forced or even paid for in the past.

In the midst of such compelling destiny evidence, intimidation cannot overtake you. As long as you keep your "new eyes" on the prize, you will find yourself virtually unable to utter the anthems of the defeated:

- "I can't do this."

- "This is impossible."

- "I guess it wasn't meant to be."

Instead you will look straight into the depths of the chasm ahead and you will knock down every wind of adversity with the anthems of a destiny believer:

- "I can't do this alone, but this *can* be done."

- "This *looks* impossible. All worthy endeavors do."

- "It wasn't meant to be easy, but this *was* meant to be. It's written in my destiny code."

Because your intention and conviction regarding destiny are become clearer, your language patterns will be altered. You will deselect vocabulary that charges the emotions with fear and doubt. Instead, you will use language as a tool—an instrument of creativity that ignites new realities and generates new possibilities.

As your speech expands beyond the boundaries of self-limitation, your experience will expand with it; in turn, bolstering your initiative and faith in desirable outcomes.

RECOGNIZING DESTINY LINKAGES

You'll remember that the starting point of destiny is your calling, which is written into your destiny code. As your destiny path becomes self-evident, you will discover surprising and meaningful linkages between this inner call, your destiny code, and your outer works. The order of discovery varies from person to person according to the specifics of their life experiences, yet the discovery process is common to all.

For example, you may have had a deep yearning to play the piano since childhood. Perhaps a piano was outside the family budget and your desire went unnourished. Suddenly as a teen, your inner calling led you to get a part-time job at a music store. Suddenly, you find yourself surrounded by relatively inexpensive electronic keyboards. And, you have a store discount!

Your destiny code was at work all along. The chronology developed based on your unique circumstances. Your part-time job wasn't your destiny. Nor did it create the calling. Yet, it reignited the calling and revealed a previously hidden step on your destiny path.

This order of discovery is not written in stone. Another youth's experience could be far different. Perhaps another child had all the needed resources available from birth. Not only was a piano a possibility, but the best of pianos was available for the asking. Music lessons, recitals, and other activities might have been the milieu of the more affluent child. Either way, destiny can flourish, and the uniqueness of the experience becomes part of a personal history able to inspire and encourage others.

SERVING YOUR GREATER PURPOSE

In whatever way your destiny unfolds, you will come to a place of self-acceptance that frees you to be comfortable in your own skin. No longer are you driven to compete or create false impressions. Instead, you get in tune with your purpose and develop a deep, profound knowledge of your calling. You are open-hearted enough to grow, yet self-assured enough to say, "I'm happy being me. This is who I was born to be."

This profound knowledge of your calling empowers you to serve life as it is presented to you. Distorted value judgments are set aside; you are able to accept people and situations as they are, without the need to control or configure life to meet your subjective specifications. You serve life as it unfolds, from an internal place of peace and fulfillment. You don't flinch when a curve ball comes your way. Instead, you make adjustments and swing hard. You realize that every pitch is an opportunity to hit the ball. You won't let possibility pass you by.

Your approach to your work will be organic rather than contrived. If you are a screenwriter, you will write because you are absorbed in your call, rather than writing a particular script so you can "make it big." For those who focus on the latter, a fundamental shift is needed. The "winning" mind-set would be, "If I keep writing and improving in my craft, the people who can bring my work to full blossom will beat a pathway to my door!"

When you are ready, the right people and opportunities will show up. So relax; keep walking on your self-evident path and continue doing what you were born to do!

Secret 5 Checkpoint

Do you identify with the piano player who discovered the electronic keyboard as a teen or the well-heeled youth who had access to the perfect instrument as a child? What is the "anthem" you "sing" as a result and is that anthem subject to change?

SECRET 6
You Access the Place of Permission

With a solid path under your feet, you can see the future unfolding before your eyes. The destiny secrets that were once hidden in your heart are being made manifest in your conduct and results. As your life's picture becomes increasingly clear, your intuitive intelligence is finer tuned. It moves to the forefront and becomes more trustworthy. You gain the confidence to "go with your gut" and spend less time equivocating and second-guessing.

You nimbly intercept counter-productive anthems and actions before they produce setbacks. Therefore, you spend less time on emotional back-tracking. Your cognitive starting point in a given situation is not buried under a load of unconscious residue. Instead, you know where you stand and you move forward unencumbered.

You readily spot breaches in conscious awareness and you deftly intuit the gap between that awareness and whatever wants to emerge from beyond it. This "new business" can include revelation, understanding, unrecognized aptitudes, and destiny desires that were previously hidden in blind spots.

Because you are living a fully conscious life, you become self-facilitating. Without realizing it, you intuitively position yourself for meaningful coincidences to occur. You find yourself in the right place at the right time with the right people. Wide doors open at opportune times, precisely when you are ready to walk through them. You step across each new threshold well-prepared and full of gratitude.

This is what I call the *place of permission*. It is the environment in which you move beyond doing what you *could* do in life and into what you *would* do given the opportunity. This ideal place is not over your head or beyond your ability; you were born with the potential to operate in it.

From the place of permission, it is easier to see the connectedness of your life's circumstances and experiences. You recognize the fertile ground in which you have been placed and you operate, for the most part, unhindered in the expression of your complete person. Your giftedness finds the milieu in which it can flourish. Therefore, your dreams can be fleshed out.

The place of permission engenders a sense of fulfillment that enriches your life and brings fulfillment to others. No longer are you serving a self-centered what's-in-it-for-me mentality. In this fertile, open place, your efforts are focused on a nobler, higher purpose rather than a zero-sum quest to come out on top. The organic approach to your work described in Secret 5 reaches its fullest expression in the place of permission.

Secret 6 Checkpoint

Apply the features of Secret 6 to the specific nature of your destiny path. How might the open-heartedness described in Secret 5 interact with the fertile, open environment of the place of permission to produce the outcomes you desire?

SECRET 7
YOU CONNECT SYMBIOTICALLY WITH SIGNIFICANT OTHERS

While it is true that other people are not responsible for your destiny fulfillment, it is also true that no one achieves destiny alone.

The balance between these two statements is found in our seventh and final secret concerning the importance of having healthy, symbiotic relationships with the people who are linked to your destiny fulfillment. These are the folks with whom you share key portions of your destiny pathway, the folks who also share their path with you.

George Burns and Gracie Allen...John Lennon and Paul McCartney...and other well-known partnerships are examples of destiny achievers drawn together for destiny purposes. Not all significant relationships involve prominent partners. Many are mentor-mentee relationships such as those believed to have been shared between Isaac Asimov and Gene Rodenberry and Andrew Carnegie and Charles Schwab.[1]

It is easy to see how such relationships contribute to destiny fulfillment. The degree to which they depend on each person's inner congruence may be less apparent. The fact is that, whatever the endeavor, we are at cross-purposes with ourselves when the unconscious mind issues the mixed signals of a divided vision.

Locked into a one-step-forward-two-steps-back lifestyle, we are less likely to benefit fully from the symbiotic relationships that are supportive of destiny fulfillment. In reality, the unfinished business that drives us to satisfy unmet needs and protect our comfort zones will also draw us to people who feed on and into our neediness. These relationships breed co-dependency and diminishment of authentic identity. With identity muddied, destiny becomes more obscure.

However, when we are internally congruent so that our beliefs, thoughts, and desires line up with our choices and actions, we enter relationships for the right reasons. Because these dealings are built upon a sound foundation, they are congruous with unfolding destiny. We naturally attract and are attracted to those with whom we are to share the destiny path.

You may already have this kind of relationship with a significant person in your life. If so, you have opened yourself to this individual's input. You invite them to offer advice and correction, knowing that their guidance may cause discomfort at times. Because you are open-hearted rather than self-protective, you are not seeking those who will pump up your ego, but those who will call a spade a spade and inspire your personal growth.

Leaders will seek to connect with you because part of their destiny is to leave a legacy. As you hold yourself accountable to these symbiotic relationships, both you and your mentors will benefit. Although you are not dependent upon one another, your steps are entwined, each party making personal progress independently and in shared ways.

Those in your inner circle and those in the overall network you establish are the people who inhabit your invisible field of dreams. They are part of the answer to creating your future and you are part of the answer to creating theirs. They often provide the missing pieces for which you have searched without success.

Although your destiny code has existed all along, these folks seem to show up suddenly. Often, they are the very people you have longed to meet, but never felt worthy to engage. Before your esteem was settled in your own heart and mind, you were not ready to receive what they had to give. In fact, you may have fabricated unconscious reasons for avoiding them. And if you did connect before you were emotionally ready, you may have pushed them away altogether. In one way or another, you felt intimidated by them—until now.

Secret 7 Checkpoint

Who are the players on your invisible field of dreams? How have they contributed to your unfolding destiny so far?

As you continue to work through unfinished business and unconscious tendencies, you become comfortable with those who once seemed too "big" to enter your circle. You are at ease with them because you are becoming comfortable in your own skin. The less encumbered by self-doubt these relationships become, the more value they yield.

"Suddenly" you are where you always dreamed of being. You are transparent and able to glean from those whose accomplishments speak to your future. You come to know (you learn) as you have been known (as you have allowed others to know you).

With vibrant relationships like these in place, the unfolding of destiny becomes charged with certainty. You begin to take steps by leaps and bounds instead of by painstaking inches. Your life catches up with your destiny code at warp speed. At times, it will be hard to imagine how life changed so quickly—and so much for the better!

ENDNOTE

1. "Andrew Carnegie—A Greater Than One Leadership Profile," studentlinc (November 26, 2005), (adapted from *Maximum Impact Leadership Fax. Injoy Ministries.* 1996) http://studentlinc.typepad.com/studentlinc/2005/11/andrew_carnegie.html<http://studentlinc.typepad.com/studentlinc/2005/11/andrew_carnegie.html> (accessed January 11, 2010).

Unfold Your Destiny

1. Describe the portions of your destiny path that are already self-evident. How eager are you to take steps onto the unknown portion of your path (remember the Indiana Jones example)? Explain how your eagerness (or reticence) may be affecting your outcomes.

2. Evaluate the level at which your intuition is currently operating. What does your answer tell you about the clarity of your life's bigger picture?

3. Name those people whom you believe would be apt mentors. Explain why you feel this way about them. Describe the degree to which you feel worthy of their interest. Consider the deeper implications of your response.

CHAPTER ELEVEN heading

CHAPTER ELEVEN

Ride This Pony Home

"We must be willing to get rid
of the life we've planned, so as to have
the life that is waiting for us."
—Joseph Campbell

WITH THE TURN OF every page, you have been marching toward your destiny. Step by step, you have plumbed the depths in search of truth and aligned your reality with what is, in the most profound sense of the word, *authentic.*

The reality you are seeking is genuine in every way. It is the most expansive picture of your life, a vision based in the truth of two inseparable elements of your person: your authentic identity and your God-given destiny. It is a reality, not of secrets kept, but of secrets revealed, a safe place of transparency and ownership that exists outside the confines of a comfort zone.

This reality is one in which preconceived notions are confronted with honesty and discarded when examination proves them to be inaccurate. Malformed concepts such as *I can't...I am less than...Whatever happens, happens...*are exposed, challenged, and rooted out. In this reality, your unconscious mind is called to account and your conscious mind is restored to its intended role. It is once again free to serve you, the natural-born meaning-maker, as you exert upon your circumstances and your world the influence you were born to wield.

The reality we have explored together is an environment that supports destiny fulfillment. It is the spiritual, emotional, and cognitive place where the inborn quest for meaning is embraced rather than marginalized. It is a healthy atmosphere in which you keep no secrets from yourself; instead you are willing to look under life's mossy rocks to uncover the fallacies and misguided attitudes that once prompted you to accept false boundaries.

In this destiny environment, the unconscious mind needn't flail about, wondering why you're here. The wondering is over and the time of meaning making is here. Your conscious mind forms and owns the fundamental question all of us must have answered: *Who am I, really?* You ask, not rhetorically, but because you know that the answer is weighty. It is more than a tidbit of information; it is a master key to unfolding destiny.

You ask because you understand that your quest for meaning will reveal your purpose. You know that this purpose was written into your destiny code long before you knew such a code existed. You realize that this code powers the engines of destiny fulfillment and reveals the providential connectedness of things you thought were insufferably random.

Suddenly, the patchwork of unexpected roadblocks, misunderstandings, longings, crises, setbacks, and ecstasies has meaning. You can gaze behind you and see how the seemingly mismatched threads of your existence are arranged masterfully to produce a perfectly balanced, beautifully composed, one-of-a-kind tapestry.

Your page-by-page journey through this book and into your own heart has reminded you of the power of your imagination to create something—even elements of your future—out of nothing more than a revelation of the providential plan for your life. The belief that life's outcomes are out of your hands has been updated with the truth that your outcomes begin in your thinking.

The knowledge that every destiny that you need you have is already available generates the freedom to step outside the borders of *what is* into the unexplored territory of *what can be.* The curtains have been drawn back and light is streaming in. You can see the big picture. You are taking your destiny inventory, deciding what stays and what goes, which behaviors and perspectives serve the interests of your life's grand design and which keep you tethered to Point A.

In the territory of unfolding destiny, you are relieved of the burdens of performance mentality and emotional cover-ups. You are severed from the tentacles of a false and falsely created self-image and released into the acceptance of your own self-worth. No longer will you exchange authenticity for a short-lived jolt of self-esteem. The trait of self-esteem has been uncovered and fortified. The skill of self-esteem is being sharpened as you learn to move through and master the process of unfolding destiny.

Your way of being is restored to wholeness as your uniqueness is honored and exposed to the light. As a result, all that is within you is free to emerge; you are both being and becoming the person you were created to be. Because the real you is interacting with others, they draw strength from who you are. Because your destiny is unfolding, those around you are freer to become the people they were created to be.

Living from the inside out is your lifestyle. You understand the power of connecting your inner values and core criteria with the outer dreams, goals, objectives, and outcomes that you envision. You are aware of the vitality generated by your destiny-driven intentions and passions. You recognize the value of your life story, personal history, and changing life seasons. Acceptance has liberated you to live unencumbered by the fear of rejection; therefore you find strength in owning your past. Instead of a painful reminder of darker days, it is a testimony to the fullness of your destiny, a chronicle in which even the tear-stained pages are valuable.

The power of value-judging that once held sway over your best intentions has been effectively neutralized. Yes, this is a lifelong journey and you will have countless opportunities to succumb to this unconscious activity in the days to come. But it need never catch you unaware again. Your renewed, fully conscious approach to life will expose every unconscious pitfall and keep you from sowing and reaping illegitimate verdicts. Instead, you will give and receive affirmation, meeting your needs and the needs of others and helping to free everyone involved from a life of approval addiction.

On the path of unfolding destiny, the lifestyle of forgiveness is embraced and the act of forgiving is recognized for what it is: a healing balm that releases offender and offended from the present and future torment of what has already been locked in the past. Most important of all, you forgive and love yourself unconditionally.

All this is happening and more. In digging your way to the core of your life and beliefs, you have found some treasures. You have held many of them up to the light. Some are yet to be unearthed. You will soon marvel at those jewels, too. Without "warning," you will experience a genuine, authentic, destiny-based empowerment you have never known.

Perhaps you already have.

THE SEVEN SECRETS IN REAL TIME

You have amassed a wealth of information and insight. But, have you noticed that life doesn't stop for the learning process or wait for you to implement all you've learned?

No problem there! The seven secrets aren't about studying life in a test tube. They are about getting your hands dirty and your destiny juices flowing as you investigate the vast field of opportunities surrounding you. Your quest for destiny will take some legwork and some elbow grease.

The secrets are perfectly suited for such a working environment. They travel with you moment by moment and place to place, ready to be lived. Every crisis of meaning and process you activate is your training ground. Therefore, wherever you are is where you need to be. Your next step starts here.

From this point onward, consider yourself appointed to live in the moment and consciously walk your destiny path. Your assignment will require a willingness to make and own mistakes and accept an often imperfect reality. But know this: your life is going somewhere, and it is changing for the better. You have big things ahead, so never…never…ever quit.

No longer is destiny someone else's domain. It's not for some-one more special, more gifted, more capable, more lovable, or more favored. *You* are that someone! The seven secrets apply to you as much as they apply to the scores of destiny achievers I have studied over the years. Whether we are talking about Alexander the Great or Alexander Solzhenitsyn, Jane Goodall or Jane Austen, the secrets are the same. More importantly, the activation of destiny DNA is as available to you as it was to them. They were not immortal figures to whom fictitious mythical powers were assigned. They were flesh-and-blood human beings with flaws, fears, foibles—and profound contributions to make.

They just happened to know the things you now know. They learned by experience that extraordinary destinies unfold in the crises and processes of ordinary life. They found out that even the chaotic experiences of their lives weren't random. At some point, the destiny path became clear to them, as it does to all great men and women. Day by day, they followed the part of the path they could see. One step at a time, they saw where the next footfall would land.

Incrementally, they reached the place of permission where they operated unhindered in the expression of their personhood and gift-edness. There, they served a higher and nobler purpose than them-selves and brought fulfillment to others. Notwithstanding their ingenuity and talent, they connected symbiotically with others who would contribute to the cause of their destinies.

All of it happened in their lives as it is happening in yours—in real time.

The Torch Is Passed

You have in your hands the golden nuggets all destiny achievers have learned. These principles will produce transformation if you embrace them. Live them in real time, when you are showered with blessings and when you are up to your neck in alligators. Remind yourself of the principles often. Wear the pages of this book to shreds, if necessary.

Whatever you do, find in every experience the kernel of destiny waiting to be released and value it. Let truth invade your heart every day of your life and invite others to share the destiny path with you.

Stay saddled up. You have a destiny to unfold!

For More Information

For more information about Mark Chironna visit:
www.MarkChironna.com.